ANTI-INFLAMM
COOKBOOK
FOR BEGINNERS
2024

Achieve Wellness With More Than 2000 Days Of
Tasty, Easy-To-Follow Recipes That Reduce
Inflammation And Energize Your Life

Zelda Fleming

4

TABLE OF CONTENTS

LIGHT AND REFRESHING OPTIONS 94

INDULGENT DESSERTS 96

CHAPTER 10: 30-DAY MEAL PLAN 99

CHAPTER 11: TIPS FOR LONG-TERM SUCCESS 103

APPENDIX 109

A SPECIAL THANK YOU 117

INTRODUCTION

WELCOME TO YOUR JOURNEY TO WELLNESS

Embarking on the path to rejuvenated health through nutrition is more than a diet change; it's a heartfelt commitment to transforming your life, embracing wellness, and engaging with every meal in a profoundly nurturing way. As you hold this book in your hands, imagine it as a trustworthy companion on your journey towards an invigorated, inflammation-free existence.

The term 'wellness' often conjures images of serene yoga studios or the calming shores of a remote lake at sunrise. However, the true essence of wellness begins from within, specifically within the very foods we consume. The commitment you're about to make — towards an anti-inflammatory lifestyle — is not merely about avoiding certain discomforts but nurturing your body to its optimal state. Think of it as forging a beautiful alliance with food, where each ingredient you select contributes to a symphony of health benefits.

Understanding inflammation, as you will soon discover in the profound pages of this book, isn't just about recognizing what goes wrong when our bodies struggle but appreciating the incredible potential for transformation that lies in our dietary choices. Inflammation is the body's natural response to protect itself against harm, but when it becomes chronic, it can lead to various health issues, leaving you feeling constantly drained and unwell. This is where your journey with our anti-inflammatory cookbook begins — transitioning from understanding to action.

The road map laid out in these pages is designed not only to guide you but also to empower and enlighten. We'll delve into the science of anti-inflammatory foods, demystifying the nutritional aspects and showcasing how you can harness these properties to cater to your body's needs. Remember, every body is unique, and therefore, understanding the nuances of how these foods interact with your unique biological makeup is critical.

Transitioning to an anti-inflammatory diet isn't about stringent restrictions or overwhelming changes. Instead, it's about making thoughtful, incremental adjustments that cumulatively transform your diet and, ultimately, your life. It's akin to learning a new language — at first, it seems foreign and challenging, but with practice, it becomes a natural, fluid form of communication. Here, your new dialect is the language of healing foods, spoken through each anti-inflammatory dish you prepare.

Picture the changes you'll undertake not as giving up what you love, but as discovering new foods and flavors that love you back. It's about expanding your palette and culinary skills while your body reaps the benefits of wholesome, nutrient-dense foods. Every chapter to follow is filled with more than just recipes; they are your stepping stones to a vibrant, healthier life.

Throughout this book, you'll encounter stories from individuals just like you — those who felt bogged down by inflammation and fatigue and found renewal through the power of their plates. These accounts are not only here to inspire but to remind you that you're not alone on this journey. Many have walked this path and have turned their lives around, one meal at a time.

Moreover, as we traverse through the pages of practical guidance and mouthwatering recipes, remember that this journey is also about grace and patience. Changes to your diet, like any good habit, require time to take root and flourish. Some days will be easier, and some will be challenging, but each step is a progress towards a fervently sought-after destination — better health and enhanced well-being.

Now, as you begin, consider how your meals can become a focal point for change. Each ingredient, each method of preparation you learn holds the potential to decrease inflammation in your body, giving you more days filled with energy and joy. You'll find that even on a busy weeknight, a simple, nutritious meal can be a powerful act of self-care.

As we proceed, keep in mind that the structure of this book is crafted to gradually build your knowledge and skills. We start simple, laying the groundwork, and gradually move towards more complex meals and concepts. This is to ensure that as your confidence grows, so does your capability to mix, match, and adapt recipes to suit your taste buds and nutritional needs.

There's an old saying that the journey of a thousand miles begins with a single step. Today, as you turn these pages, you take that step — not just towards cooking but towards a rejuvenated self. Let this cookbook be your guide, your inspiration, and your companion as you rediscover the joy of eating for health. Welcome to your journey to wellness — may it be as delightful as it is transformative.

UNDERSTANDING INFLAMMATION

To truly embark on a journey of healing and wellness through your diet, it's important to understand the underpinnings of what you're mitigating—namely, inflammation. But what exactly is inflammation? Often painted in a negative light, it's actually a critical process, an inherent part of the body's own defense mechanism. Imagine, if you will, inflammation as your body's vigilant protector, springing into action to shield and heal you from bacterial invasions or injuries. However, when this protective flame burns too intensely or lingers too long, it becomes a fire that can damage the body it was meant to protect.

Let's delve deeper into the dual nature of inflammation: acute and chronic. Acronym aside, acute inflammation is your body's immediate and temporary response to an injury or illness. Picture this scenario—a splinter in your finger. It hurts and swells up, right? That's acute inflammation working to isolate and expel the foreign intruder. Normally, this response dissipates as healing completes, a perfect example of inflammation as a beneficial soldier in the body's army.

However, the story shifts when we talk about chronic inflammation. This form isn't as overt as an inflamed cut or bruised skin. It's insidious, often silent for a long time, lurking in the body. This type of inflammation can be triggered by numerous factors including chronic stress, lingering infections, autoimmune disorders, and, significantly, our diets.

Here we connect the dots to why an anti-inflammatory diet is more than a trend—it's a profound tool. You see, regular consumption of certain foods has been found to perpetually provoke the body's inflammatory process. Imagine tossing a small, barely noticeable log on a fire each night. Eventually, you'll have a fierce fire. In the body, this relentless inflammation may lead to a host of diseases like arthritis, heart disease, Alzheimer's, and more. It affects your vitality, your energy, and your zest for life.

But, there's a silver lining in this cloudy scenario. Just as diet can induce chronic inflammation, it can also be the most powerful remedy to reduce and prevent it. Our focus here is to explore how shifting our eating habits can quench this persistent inflammation—like removing logs from the fire, one by one.

Think of anti-inflammatory eating not as a diet in the conventional sense of the word but as a change in lifestyle, a dedication to nourishing your body with foods that are as close to their natural state as possible—rich in antioxidants, devoid of artificial ingredients, low in sugars, and high in omega-3 fatty acids. These nutrients are like your body's own fire extinguishers, effectively damping down inflammatory responses.

Yet, this lifestyle adjustment doesn't mean simply avoiding junk food; it's about creating a delicious, diverse menu from vegetables, fruits, herbs, spices, nuts, and whole grains—foods that are celebrated not only for their ability to fight inflammation but for their myriad other health benefits, including heart health, cognitive function, and overall vitality.

Engaging with your food at this deeper level opens up a beautiful rhythm of eating—where each meal supports your health in more ways than one. It transforms your relationship with food. You're no longer eating solely to satisfy hunger, but to heal, to rejuvenate, and to thrive. With each chapter, as we dissect these food groups and learn how they contribute to reducing inflammation, you'll gain the tools and knowledge to curate your own nutritious meals consciously.

At this point, you might wonder how you'll translate this knowledge into daily habits. Think about the slow but sure steps of integrating these inflammation-soothing foods into your life. You don't need to overhaul your kitchen in one day. Instead, think of each meal as an opportunity to add something anti-inflammatory into the mix, whether it's sprinkling some turmeric on your roasted vegetables, opting for a handful of berries for a snack, or swapping out your usual cooking oil for a splash of olive oil.

By understanding inflammation and its impact on the body, and by learning how we can effectively manage it through our diet, we empower ourselves with the knowledge to make informed decisions about our health. This isn't just about avoiding discomfort or disease—this is about thriving, finding energy, and experiencing joy in a life well-nurtured by the very foods we eat.

Let this knowledge be your foundation as you move through the book, discover recipes, and harness the power of an anti-inflammatory lifestyle. This transformation is both a science and an art—equally logical and personal, demanding thoughtful consideration of how we fuel our bodies and spirits.

THE SCIENCE BEHIND ANTI-INFLAMMATORY FOODS

Peering into the science behind anti-inflammatory foods unveils a fascinating interplay between nature's bounty and our bodies, a testament to the power of diet over health. In this journey through the biological impacts of what we eat, you'll uncover why certain foods have the ability to soothe inflammation, while others provoke it. Understanding the mechanisms can transform the way you view your meals and revolutionize your approach to eating.

The principal actors in the narrative of inflammation are the various bioactive compounds naturally occurring in foods. These compounds engage with the body's cellular machinery, coaxing it towards healing and regeneration, or in unfortunate cases, causing it to react with defensive inflammation. The anti-inflammatory diet focuses predominantly on the former, encouraging the intake of foods enriched with nutrients that are known allies in the quest to quench inflammatory responses.

Omega-3 Fatty Acids—often highlighted heroes in the anti-inflammatory diet—deserve special mention. Found abundantly in fish like salmon and mackerel, as well as in flaxseed and walnuts, omega-3s are lauded for their ability to reduce the production of molecules and substances linked to inflammation, such as eicosanoids and cytokines. Research illustrates how these fatty acids help lower the levels of inflammatory markers in the body, which is why incorporating them into your diet can be particularly beneficial for inflammatory conditions like arthritis.

Antioxidants, another cornerstone of anti-inflammatory foods, play a crucial role in neutralizing free radicals—unstable molecules that can cause oxidative stress and damage cells, leading to chronic inflammation. Foods rich in antioxidants, such as berries, leafy greens, and dark chocolate, provide a defense squad equipped to combat this oxidative stress, thereby potentially reducing the overall inflammatory response in the body.

Polyphenols, a diverse group of compounds abundant in a variety of plant foods, also take a central stage. Found in everything from olive oil to dark chocolate and red wine, polyphenols can inhibit inflammation-signaling pathways within the body. Their effect is nuanced, influencing a wide array of cellular activities that promote inflammation reduction. This is particularly evident in the way certain polyphenols can modulate the immune system to prevent overactive inflammatory responses while still maintaining the body's ability to fight off diseases.

Understanding the interaction between these compounds and our body's biological systems starts with the gut, our first line of defense against pathogens and a significant source of immune activity. An anti-inflammatory diet promotes gut health by fostering a diverse and robust microbiome—the collection of friendly bacteria residing in our intestinal tract. These microorganisms play a critical role in digesting food, synthesizing nutrients, and guarding against pathogens. They also help break down dietary fibers, which can lead to the production of short-chain fatty acids known to reduce inflammation. Thus, a diet rich in varied fibers, from sources like vegetables, fruits, and whole grains, not only supports gut health but indirectly curtails inflammation.

Equally important is recognizing foods that induce inflammation to be notably minimized or avoided. For instance, excessive sugars and refined carbs can provoke rapid spikes in blood sugar, leading to an inflammatory response. Similarly, trans fats found in certain processed foods can elevate harmful LDL cholesterol levels and inflammation. By understanding these effects, you can make more informed choices, selecting foods that contribute to a soothing, rather than aggravating, bodily environment.

Moreover, spices and herbs—nature's own medicine cabinet—offer impressive anti-inflammatory properties. Turmeric, for instance, contains curcumin, a compound with strong anti-inflammatory capabilities that is as effective as some anti-inflammatory drugs. Ginger, garlic, and cinnamon also play similar roles, reducing inflammation through their powerful bioactive compounds.

In weaving this tapestry of food science into your daily eating habits, it's essential to consider not just the individual ingredients but the symphony they create together. Meal composition, timing, and even food pairings can influence how effectively these nutrients are utilized by the body. For example, pairing fat-soluble vitamins with healthy fats can maximize their absorption and enhance their anti-inflammatory effects.

By evolving your kitchen from a place of mere food preparation to a laboratory where meals are mindfully crafted to combat inflammation, you embark on a proactive route to health. Each meal becomes an opportunity to positively influence your body's inflammatory processes, helping you lead a healthier, more vibrant life.

As you turn the pages ahead and explore the recipes and strategies, let this scientific guidance be a beacon that helps you navigate the vast and sometimes confusing landscape of nutrition and health. The clarity that comes from understanding the science behind anti-inflammatory foods will empower you, transforming your approach to eating from one of restriction to one of rich, nourishing abundance. Herein lies the path to not just managing wellness, but thriving through it.

HOW TO USE THIS BOOK

Welcome to a transformative journey that extends beyond simple meal preparation to reshaping your entire lifestyle for optimal health and well-being. Considering this book as not merely a collection of recipes but as an essential guide to an anti-inflammatory lifestyle will enhance your journey. Each page aims to equip you with knowledge and tools, enabling you to easily incorporate inflammation-soothing practices into every meal you prepare.

Navigating this book is akin to embarking on a culinary adventure with a purpose. It begins with laying the theoretical groundwork in the Introduction, familiarizing you with the foundational aspects of inflammation and its dietary impacts. As you progress, the subsequent chapters break down the anti-inflammatory diet into tangible, appetizing components—from breakfast ideas to sumptuous dinners and everything in between.

Approach Each Chapter with Intent

Dive into each chapter with the intent to understand and absorb not just the 'how' but the 'why'. The flow of the book is carefully designed to build your understanding incrementally, leading from basic concepts to more nuanced aspects of the anti-inflammatory diet.

Adapt Recipes to Suit Your Needs

The recipes presented are not just instructions to be followed but are starting points for experimentation. Each recipe is flexible, encouraging you to adjust spices, substitute ingredients, and alter cooking methods based on your personal preferences and dietary needs. This adaptability makes it effortless to maintain this healthy eating pattern without feeling restricted by your culinary options.

Use the Glossary for Quick References

When encountering unfamiliar terms or ingredients, turn to the glossary section. It's crafted to be your quick go-to resource for immediate definitions and explanations, ensuring that you never feel lost or overwhelmed.

Implement Incremental Changes

Consider focusing on one recipe or chapter at a time, especially if you're new to the concepts and cooking techniques discussed. Gradual implementation fosters a more sustainable transition and helps embed these new eating habits into your long-term routine.

Engage with the Tips and Side Notes

Throughout the book, look out for tips and side notes that offer additional insight into maximizing the benefits of your meals. These could range from nutritional advice about particular ingredients to practical kitchen hacks, enhancing both the ease and enjoyment of your cooking experience.

Reflect on Your Progress

A section on reflection is also included to help you assess your journey, understand what works, and identify areas needing adjustment. Use this as an opportunity to fine-tune your approach, celebrate successes, and set goals for continued improvement.

Plan with the 30-Day Meal Planner

For structured guidance, utilize the 30-day meal plan provided in Chapter 10. It serves as an excellent basis for beginners to plan their month's meals, ensuring a balanced intake of nutrients while adhering to the anti-inflammatory guidelines. Over time, you may use the templates provided as a framework to create your own plans, based on the recipes and knowledge accumulated from earlier chapters.

Stay Informed with Resources for Further Reading

Finally, the Resources for Further Reading section acts as a bridge connecting your newly acquired knowledge with deeper dives into specific topics of interest. Whether you're looking to understand more about nutrient-dense foods or explore advanced culinary techniques, these resources can guide your continuous learning.

By engaging with this book as both a recipe collection and an educational tool, you empower yourself to make informed decisions about your diet and health. The journey you are on is personal and unique—no two paths to wellness are the same. Thus, adjust the pace and focus as needed, ensuring it completely resonates with your lifestyle, preferences, and health goals.

Remember, the journey to reduced inflammation and enhanced vitality is ongoing. Each meal, each recipe, and each day is a step forward in this nourishing voyage. With this book in hand, you're equipped not just with recipes, but with a roadmap to a healthier, more vibrant life. Utilize it as a compass, guiding you through choices and changes towards an ultimately fulfilling and inflammatory-conscious lifestyle.

CHAPTER 1: THE BASICS OF AN ANTI-INFLAMMATORY DIET

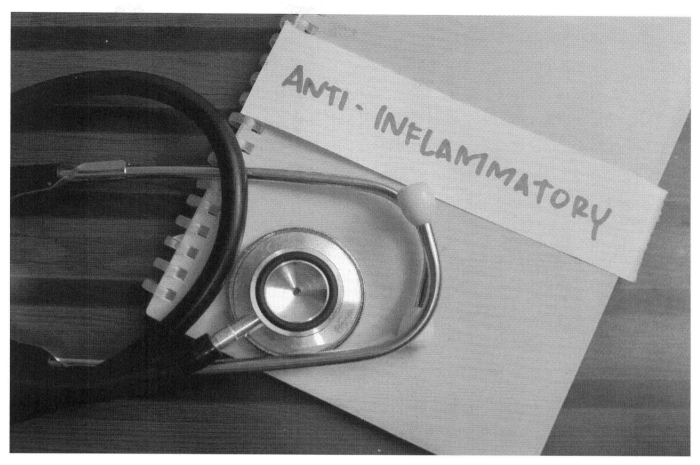

Imagine waking up each morning, feeling rejuvenated, with a vibrant energy that carries you through the day. Now, visualize achieving this via the simple magic of what's on your plate. Welcome to the journey of the Anti-Inflammatory Diet, a pathway not just toward better health, but a new way of experiencing life.

At the heart of this health revolution lies inflammation—a natural process that helps your body fight off diseases but, when out of control, can contribute to a myriad of chronic conditions, from arthritis to heart disease, depression to diabetes. The good news? Much of this is within your control, and it starts with what you eat.

The Anti-Inflammatory Diet is not a trendy regime that comes and goes but is grounded in the timeless wisdom of consuming whole, nutrient-rich foods. This means embracing colorful fruits and vegetables, whole grains, legumes, lean protein, and heart-healthy fats—all of which work harmoniously to quell inflammation and heal our bodies from the inside out.

However, transitioning to an anti-inflammatory diet doesn't mean merely swapping a few meals or resisting certain indulgences. It's about framing a new perspective on how we view and interact with food. It teaches us that food can be both medicinal and delicious, and each meal is an opportunity to heal, nourish, and revitalize our bodies.

As we embark on this chapter, you'll gain a deeper understanding of what inflammation is really about, explore the myriad health benefits of adopting an anti-inflammatory way of eating, and learn which foods to embrace and those to avoid. Through this knowledge, you'll be equipped not just with theoretical insight but with practical wisdom that paves the way for lasting health improvements.

This is just the beginning of your journey—a journey that goes beyond mere diet alterations. It's a lifelong commitment to nurturing your body and embracing a lifestyle that promotes optimal health. Let's step forward together, with each meal bringing you closer to a more vibrant, healthier version of yourself.

WHAT IS INFLAMMATION?

Imagine your body as a complex and highly efficient ecosystem continually adjusting to various internal and external stimuli. In this world, inflammation is like the emergency response team—vital and indispensable in times of genuine threats, such as infections or injuries. Yet, when this response lingers longer than necessary, it doesn't just protect—it can turn destructive.

Inflammation is derived from the Latin word *inflammare*, which means to set on fire. True to its name, inflammation can literally feel like a fire inside your body, manifesting as swelling, redness, heat, and pain. Ideally, this reaction serves as your body's natural defense mechanism against injuries or infections. When a threat is detected, your immune system responds by activating substances that protect tissues. This process is naturally expected to shut down once the healing process is complete.

However, the flame of inflammation becomes problematic when it doesn't extinguish but continues to burn. This chronic, low-grade inflammation silently damages your body, contributing to heart diseases, diabetes, arthritis, and many other chronic conditions, often without any overt symptoms.

Chronic inflammation often begins with habits or environmental factors that wouldn't seem immediately alarming—from consuming highly processed foods to persistent stress or exposure to pollutants. Imagine slowly dripping a seemingly harmless substance into a pure glass of water; over time, the substance begins to alter the water's composition. Similarly, small, persistent inflammatory triggers can fundamentally alter your body's functioning.

For many, this realization comes as a paradigm shift. Inflammation is not exclusively the swelling you feel when you stub your toe, nor is it always the redness or heat emanating from an infected wound. Indeed, inflammation often operates far beneath this threshold of sensation, weaving stealthily into your organs and systems, catalyzing subtle yet significant changes in your health over time.

Ironically, the diet—our everyday tool for sustenance—plays a monumental role in modulating inflammation. Some foods, like sugary treats and fried items, can provoke inflammatory processes. They are like throwing gasoline on the fire, creating flare-ups that our body struggles to control. On the other hand, foods rich in omega-3 fatty acids, antioxidants, and fiber act like a cooling salve that soothes this inflammatory fire.

Furthermore, studies increasingly underline how our dietary choices influence microorganisms in our gut, which in turn affect our immune system and its propensity towards inflammation. A healthy gut flora energized by fiber-rich, nutrient-dense foods supports an effective and balanced immune response, thereby dampening inflammation.

Genetics also plays a role, scripting how our bodies might react to these inflammatory triggers. However, the narrative of genetics is far from being absolute. Epigenetics, the study of how your behaviors and environment can cause changes that affect the way your genes work, is also crucial. Unlike genetic changes, epigenetic changes are reversible and can be influenced over time, largely through lifestyle choices including diet, activity, and stress management.

Addressing inflammation is thus not only about adjusting what we eat but also modifying how we live. It involves tuning in to our bodies' rhythms, respecting its signals of distress, and proactively cultivating habits that mitigate harmful inflammatory responses.

Consider the act of managing inflammation through diet as cultivating a garden. Just as a garden thrives with the right balance of sunlight, water, and nutrients, our bodies flourish when nourished with the correct balance of foods. Anti-inflammatory eating is about creating an internal environment where wellness can blossom, rooted in the understanding that each meal can act as a dose of prevention or a contributing factor to chronic inflammation.

Let's take, for example, the humble blueberry, brimming with vitamins, antioxidants, and phytoflavones—each component playing a symphony that calms inflammatory markers, promotes heart health, and shields the body against oxidative stress. Or consider the power of turmeric, a vibrant spice with curcumin, known for its profound anti-inflammatory effects, so potent that it matches the effectiveness of some anti-inflammatory drugs.

Understanding inflammation in its dual role—as protector and potential perpetrator—lays a foundational step in adopting an anti-inflammatory lifestyle. This knowledge empowers you to make informed decisions, not out of fear but from a place of awareness and control.

As we delve deeper into the principles of anti-inflammatory eating, remember that this journey is deeply personal. What works as a soothing balm for one might not have the same effect for another. Thus, embarking on this path is not merely about following a set of dietary guidelines but about listening to, understanding, and gently reshaping your body's response to what you eat and how you live your life.

BENEFITS OF AN ANTI-INFLAMMATORY DIET

Embarking on an anti-inflammatory diet is much like turning a skilled gardener's attention to a neglected patch of earth. The results aren't immediate, but the gradual nurturing brings a bounty of health benefits that are both visible and unseen. The transformative powers of this diet stretch across various aspects of health, offering a more vibrant, energetic, and balanced life.

First and foremost, adopting an anti-inflammatory diet enhances heart health. Cardiovascular diseases, which stand as leading causes of morbidity globally, are significantly underpinned by chronic inflammation. Foods rich in antioxidants, unsaturated fats, and fiber—hallmarks of the anti-inflammatory protocol—act to dilute and disarm the inflammatory processes that precipitate heart disease. Take, for example, the simple act of replacing butter with olive oil, which embodies mono-unsaturated fats known to decrease LDL (bad cholesterol) levels, thereby reducing the risk of stroke and heart attack.

Beyond the heart, the benefits cascade to our joints and muscles. Inflammatory conditions such as arthritis see a notable reduction in symptoms when the diet shifts towards anti-inflammatory foods. Omega-3 fatty acids, found abundantly in fish like salmon and in flaxseeds, are instrumental in reducing joint stiffness and pain. These foods work at a molecular level to inhibit the inflammatory pathways, offering relief and increased mobility in individuals suffering from rheumatic diseases.

The brain, too, is a significant benefactor of this dietary shift. Chronic inflammation is a recognized culprit in the development of neurodegenerative diseases such as Alzheimer's and Parkinson's. Diets rich in leafy greens, nuts, berries, and fatty fish have been shown to lower the risk of cognitive decline. These foods boost brain health not just through their anti-inflammatory actions but also by enhancing brain plasticity, which improves memory and learning.

On a cellular level, the impact of an anti-inflammatory diet is profound. Inflammation can accelerate the aging process by promoting oxidative stress and cellular damage. Antioxidant-rich foods such as berries, nuts, and spices like turmeric counter this effect, thus playing a role in cell repair and longevity. This cellular 'tune-up' manifests outwardly too—healthier skin, fewer wrinkles, and a more youthful appearance often follow an anti-inflammatory lifestyle.

Moreover, managing weight becomes more intuitive on an anti-inflammatory diet. Highly processed foods and sugars, which contribute to weight gain and metabolic disturbances, are replaced with whole grains, proteins, and abundant vegetables that support satiety and nutrient intake without excess calories. This not only aids in weight management but also stabilizes blood sugar levels, reducing the risk of diabetes.

The psychological effects are equally compelling. Chronic inflammation has been linked to mood disorders such as depression and anxiety. By modulating the diet to reduce inflammation, many find a significant improvement in their mental health. The gut-brain axis, a critical pathway where the gastrointestinal tract and brain communicate, is influenced by the gut microbiota, which thrives on a fiber-rich, reduced-inflammatory diet, positively impacting overall mental well-being.

For those living with autoimmune diseases, where the immune system mistakenly attacks healthy cells, an anti-inflammatory diet can be particularly therapeutic. By calming inflammation, the dietary approach can help decrease flare-ups and symptom intensity across conditions such as multiple sclerosis, lupus, and inflammatory bowel diseases.

The protective effects extend even to the lungs. Chronic obstructive pulmonary disease (COPD) and asthma are linked with chronic inflammation. A diet rich in fruits, vegetables, and omega-3 fatty acids can improve lung function and reduce symptoms. This is particularly crucial for those living in urban environments with higher pollution levels, as dietary interventions can provide a buffer against the inflammatory effects of environmental toxins.

Lastly, the benefits of an anti-inflammatory diet reinforce each other, creating a positive feedback loop. Better heart health enhances your ability to exercise; weight loss reduces stress on joints and improves mobility; mental clarity boosts your motivation and engagement with healthier lifestyle choices; the cumulative effect is a holistic elevation of health.

Understanding these benefits allows us to see the anti-inflammatory diet not just as a means to manage specific symptoms, but as a comprehensive lifestyle approach that nurtures your body across all fronts. Just as a well-tended garden delights with its vitality and diversity, a body nurtured by anti-inflammatory choices rewards you with a resilience and vigor for life.

KEY COMPONENTS OF THE DIET

Navigating the world of anti-inflammatory foods may seem like venturing into a lush, diverse garden, each path promising to lead to improved health and vitality. To fully embrace and understand the components of an anti-inflammatory diet, envision stocking your pantry and refrigerator as carefully as a painter selects colors for a masterpiece, knowing that each choice contributes to the final picture of health.

The foundational building blocks of an anti-inflammatory diet are not singular magical ingredients poised to banish inflammation with a dash or spoonful. Rather, they combine synergistically, affecting body systems with a profundity that nourishes and transforms. There are several food groups and nutrients that are considered essential in this healthful approach to eating.

Fruits and Vegetables

Packed with antioxidants, vitamins, minerals, and fibers, fruits and vegetables are the cornerstones of anti-inflammatory eating. Antioxidants help reduce oxidative stress in the body, which can trigger inflammation. Vibrant berries, leafy greens, and deeply colored beets and carrots not only add color to your plate but are loaded with phytonutrients that cool inflammation. The diversity one finds in plant-based foods isn't just pleasing to the eye but is crucial for fortifying the body against the stresses that contribute to inflammation.

Whole Grains

When whole grains replace refined counterparts, the body benefits from an extended release of energy, steady insulin levels, and an influx of nutrients. Foods such as quinoa, brown rice, and whole oats are high in fiber, which can help to lower blood levels of C-reactive protein, a marker of inflammation in the body. Additionally, these grains contribute to a healthy gut microbiome, a key player in immune function and inflammation management.

Healthy Fats

The role of fats in an anti-inflammatory diet is nuanced and critical. Sources of healthy fats like avocados, olive oil, and omega-3 fatty acids found in certain fish such as salmon and mackerel, are potent anti-inflammatory agents. They assist in building cell membranes and producing hormones that regulate inflammation. Importantly, the balance between omega-6 and omega-3 fatty acids should be considered; a higher intake of omega-6s, common in the standard American diet, can promote inflammation, while omega-3s serve to reduce it.

Nuts and Seeds

Nuts and seeds are more than just a crunchy, satisfying snack. They contain a bounty of beneficial fats, protein, and fiber. Almonds, flaxseeds, and chia seeds, for instance, possess high levels of anti-inflammatory nutrients and can support heart health, reduce blood pressure, and decrease inflammation markers in the blood.

Proteins

Selecting the right types of protein is crucial on an anti-inflammatory diet. While red and processed meats are known to contribute to inflammatory processes, sources like legumes, lentils, and tofu not only offer hearty alternatives but are accompanied by fiber and other nutrients beneficial for inflammation. Fish, particularly those rich in omega-3 fatty acids, stand out for their anti-inflammatory properties, supporting brain and heart health.

Spices and Herbs

Incorporating herbs and spices into meals can turn ordinary ingredients into a powerhouse of flavor and nutrients. Many herbs and spices are revered not just for their flavor but for their medicinal properties as well. Turmeric, ginger, garlic, and cinnamon are just a few examples that have been studied for their effective anti-inflammatory properties.

Beverages

What you choose to drink can also reflect your commitment to an anti-inflammatory lifestyle. Green tea, for instance, contains epigallocatechin gallate (EGCG), a compound that research has shown to reduce inflammation and help to prevent damage to the body's cells. Similarly, beverages like water infused with lemon or herbal teas can hydrate the body while reducing inflammation, as opposed to sugary drinks which can exacerbate it.

This variety of food groups underscores a fundamental principle of the anti-inflammatory diet: diversity and balance. Just as a garden requires a balance of elements to thrive—sunlight, water, soil nutrients—so too does your body benefit from a balanced and varied diet that keeps inflammation at bay.

However, integrating these components is not just about individual ingredients; it's about creating a symphony of flavors that work together to reduce inflammation and promote overall health and well-being. Each meal is an opportunity to build on the principles of anti-inflammatory eating, translating theory into practice—one plate at a time.

As you embrace this approach, remember that the journey to reduced inflammation and improved health is gradual. Each positive choice is a step towards a healthier future, where the body is less burdened by chronic inflammation and more energized to live life to its fullest. Just like any garden, the fruits of your labor in following an anti-inflammatory diet will take time to cultivate, but the benefits will be enduring and profound, revealing themselves in your vitality and vibrancy in the years to come.

FOODS TO AVOID

Embarking on an anti-inflammatory diet invites you to reimagine your plate, filling it with a rich tapestry of nourishing, vibrant foods. However, just as important as knowing what to embrace is understanding what to leave out. Like gardeners who weed their plots to protect their plants' growth, you must identify and reduce foods that contribute to inflammation, ensuring your body's landscape can thrive.

Processed and Refined Foods

The convenience of processed foods is undeniable in our fast-paced world. Yet, these foods are often culprits in raising inflammation levels. They are typically high in unhealthy fats, added sugars, and sodium, lacking the beneficial nutrients found in whole, unprocessed foods. Consider refined carbohydrates like white bread, pastries, and other baked goods, which can trigger a spike and subsequent crash in blood sugar levels, fostering an inflammatory environment.

Sugars and Artificial Sweeteners

Sugar, particularly high-fructose corn syrup found in many sodas and sweetened beverages, promotes inflammation and has been linked to a myriad of health issues, including obesity and diabetes. Consuming excess sugar can prompt glycation, a process where sugar molecules bond to proteins or lipids, often leading to damaged cells and inflammatory responses. While artificial sweeteners offer a calorie-free alternative, they're not free from criticism. Some studies suggest they can negatively affect gut microbiota and increase glucose intolerance, subtly elevating inflammation.

Trans Fats and Certain Saturated Fats

Trans fats are particularly harmful and have been associated directly with increased inflammation, heart disease, and stroke. These fats, often listed on labels as "partially hydrogenated oils," are found in some fried foods, margarine, and snack products. Saturated fats, found in red meats and full-fat dairy products, when consumed excessively, can also contribute to inflammation. The key lies in moderation and balance, incorporating healthier fat sources, like avocados and nuts, to supplant these less desirable fats.

Omega-6 Fatty Acids

While omega-6 fatty acids are essential to health, the modern diet often has a disproportionately high amount of omega-6s compared to omega-3s. This imbalance can promote inflammation. Common sources of omega-6 fatty acids include certain vegetable oils, such as corn oil and safflower oil. Adjusting this balance by increasing omega-3 intake through foods like fish and flaxseed can help manage inflammation.

Dairy Products

For some individuals, dairy products can trigger an inflammatory response, particularly in those who are lactose intolerant or have a dairy allergy. Additionally, the high fat content in full-fat dairy products can contribute to inflammation. Alternatives like almond, soy, or oat milk can serve as suitable substitutes for those who find dairy problematic.

Alcohol

Moderate alcohol consumption might offer some health benefits, such as a potential reduced risk of heart disease. However, excessive alcohol intake can lead to a cascade of inflammatory responses throughout the body. It can disrupt gut barriers, allowing bacteria to pass into the blood more freely and potentially triggering inflammation.

Gluten and Refined Grains

For those with celiac disease or gluten sensitivity, gluten—a protein found in wheat, barley, and rye—can provoke severe inflammation. Even for individuals without these conditions, heavily refined grains can contribute to inflammation due to their low fiber content and high glycemic index, which can spike blood sugar levels.

Nightshade Vegetables

Though not universally problematic and very healthy for many, nightshade vegetables—such as tomatoes, peppers, eggplants, and potatoes—can exacerbate inflammation in some individuals. This is particularly noted in people with autoimmune diseases. Monitoring your body's response to these foods and adjusting intake accordingly can be a wise approach.

Additives and Preservatives

Artificial additives and preservatives in foods can trigger inflammatory processes in the body. These chemicals can interfere with normal bodily functions and impact the immune system. Emphasizing fresh, minimally processed foods can drastically reduce the consumption of these unnecessary and potentially harmful ingredients.

Understanding these dietary impacts requires listening to your body and observing how it responds to various foods. Inflammation can be insidious, gradually affecting your health without clear immediate signs. By keeping a food diary or working with a healthcare professional, you can identify sensitivities and adjust your diet to support your body's needs more effectively.

As you refine your diet, think of each meal as an opportunity to feed your health and starve inflammation. The task isn't merely about restriction but about remodeling your dietary landscape to foster resilience against diseases and enhance overall wellness. By making informed choices about what not to include on your plate, you empower yourself to live a healthier, more vibrant life, laying the foundation for a robust and flourishing existence.

CHAPTER 2: GETTING STARTED

Welcome to the most empowering stage of your journey: the beginning of your transition into an anti-inflammatory lifestyle. Imagine this chapter as your own culinary treasure map, where every tip and strategy guides you closer to the treasure of wellness and energy.

Embarking on an anti-inflammatory diet might feel daunting at first, reflecting a major shift from your usual eating patterns. Perhaps your kitchen shelves are still filled with foods that fuel inflammation rather than fight it. Or maybe the prospect of changing your diet seems like navigating a maze without a map. This chapter aims to serve as your compass, helping you set clear, attainable goals and equipping you with the essentials you need to start this transformative journey.

Firstly, envision what you want to achieve. Imagine waking up feeling revitalized, with your body thanking you for the nourishing foods you've eaten. Keep this vision close to your heart; it's what will keep you motivated on the days when old habits beckon.

As we progress, we'll explore how to revamp your pantry. This isn't just about removing what doesn't serve you; it's about discovering a world of flavors through anti-inflammatory staples—think vibrant spices, wholesome grains, and lush vegetables that invite creativity into your meals.

Moreover, meal planning will no longer be a chore but a delightful venture. I'll share strategies to ensure that your meal planning is not only straightforward but also enjoyable. You'll learn how to weave variety and taste into every meal, making it easier to stick to your new diet without feeling deprived.

Remember, this chapter is not just about dietary changes; it's about setting the stage for a lifelong journey of health and vitality. It's about crafting a lifestyle that allows you to thrive, not just survive. So, take a deep breath and let's step boldly together into this new chapter of your life, equipped with the knowledge and confidence to transform your diet into a powerful ally against inflammation.

SETTING YOUR GOALS

Setting your goals is like planting seeds in a garden of potential: each careful choice and clearly defined objective can blossom into health and vibrancy. When embarking on an anti-inflammatory lifestyle, your goals are not just milestones to be ticked off; they are the driving force that guides your daily actions and choices. Let's journey through the process of setting meaningful and achievable goals that will help you harness the full potential of an anti-inflammatory diet.

The Power of Clarity

Imagine stepping into a serene morning, the pathway ahead clear and the destination visible in the golden light. This vision mirrors the power of clarity in setting goals. To start, define what 'wellness' means for you. Does it involve pain-free days, more energy to enjoy life, or perhaps improved overall vitality? Identifying this end goal is essential as it anchors every decision and meal choice you make.

Make Your Goals Specific and Achievable

Goals should be as specific as possible. Instead of vaguely aiming to 'eat healthier', establish precisely what that looks like. For instance, "I will include a serving of anti-inflammatory foods like berries or leafy greens in each meal." This specificity turns the abstract into action and makes your daily decisions easier.

When identifying these goals, ensure they are achievable. It is empowering to reach critical markers along your wellness journey. If a complete diet overhaul feels overwhelming, start small. Maybe your initial goal is to incorporate an anti-inflammatory smoothie into your breakfast routine three times a week. As these smaller goals become habits, they pave the way for more significant changes.

Long-term and Short-term Goals

In your garden of goals, both long-term and short-term aspirations are valuable. Long-term goals provide a vision and a destination, such like reducing joint stiffness or improving heart health through sustained dietary changes. They are your horizon, always in view, guiding your journey.

Short-term goals, on the other hand, are the steps you climb to reach that horizon. They are immediate and tactical, such as planning your meals for the week or choosing to swap out certain oils in your cooking for healthier alternatives. Achieving these smaller, quick wins provides ongoing motivation and tangible proof of your commitment.

Aligning Goals with Daily Habits

Turning goals into reality requires them to be woven into the fabric of your daily life. Begin by examining your typical day and identifying opportunities to infuse anti-inflammatory choices. For instance, if lunch often includes a sandwich with processed meats, could you replace it with a salad rich in omega-3 fatty acids and antioxidants?

Integration like this doesn't just make the goal more achievable; it makes it a part of your identity. Each small decision contributes to a bigger picture, reinforcing your commitment to an anti-inflammatory lifestyle.

Monitoring Progress

Tracking progress is crucial. It serves as both a motivator and a form of accountability. You might choose to keep a food diary, use an app, or even maintain a simple journal detailing how you feel physically and mentally. This monitoring helps you see trends over time, providing insight into what works best for your body and lifestyle.

As you track, celebrate every success, no matter how small. Did you choose a side of vegetables instead of fries? That's a victory. Did you feel more energetic after a week of following your new diet? That's a profound reason to keep going. These celebrations fuel your journey, turning the arduous task of changing one's diet into a rewarding exploration of self-care.

Flexibility: The Key to Sustained Success

While dedication is critical, so is flexibility. Life's ebb and flow might not always align with your planned goals, and that's okay. If you miss a mark, harness the lessons learned rather than dwell on the setback. Perhaps a goal was unrealistic, or unexpected events threw you off track. Refine your goals as needed, adapting them to new circumstances and insights, just as you might adjust a recipe to better suit your taste or the ingredients available.

Community and Support

Finally, remember that you are not on this journey alone. Sharing your goals with family or a community can provide an invaluable support network. Whether it's someone to swap recipes with, a companion for grocery shopping, or simply a friend to share your successes and struggles, having support can make a significant difference in maintaining your motivation and achieving your goals.

In setting your goals, treat yourself with kindness and patience. Like any journey, transforming your diet and lifestyle is a process, one that is uniquely yours. Allow your goals to evolve with you, reflecting not only your desires for a healthier life but also celebrating who you are along the way. After all, the ultimate goal of any health journey is not just to live better but to live well, embracing each day with vitality and joy.

STOCKING YOUR PANTRY WITH ANTI-INFLAMMATORY STAPLES

Imagine turning the key in the lock and opening the door to your pantry—a sanctuary where every jar, box, and bottle supports your journey to wellness. Stocking your pantry with anti-inflammatory staples transforms it into a powerful toolkit, arming you with the essential components to nourish your body and foster health every day. When you first consider overhauling your pantry, it can feel like a daunting task. But as you remove each item that doesn't align with your new dietary choices, you're not just decluttering physical space—you're also clearing mental space, making room for new habits and healthier alternatives.

Beginning with the Basics: Oils and Fats

Transitioning to an anti-inflammatory diet means reconsidering the fats and oils that form the basis of your cooking. Oils rich in omega-3 fatty acids, like extra virgin olive oil, flaxseed oil, and walnut oil, not only enhance the flavor of your meals but also offer anti-inflammatory benefits. Swap out processed vegetable oils—often laden with omega-6 fatty acids, which can promote inflammation—for these healthier alternatives.

Whole Grains: Sustenance and Substance

Refined grains are a common culprit behind elevated inflammation levels. Instead, fill your shelves with whole grains like quinoa, brown rice, and barley. These grains provide a hearty base for meals, are rich in fiber, and help control blood sugar levels, indirectly reducing inflammation.

The Spice of Life: Anti-Inflammatory Herbs and Spices

Turmeric, ginger, garlic, and cinnamon aren't just spices—they're small packets of anti-inflammatory power. Integrating these into your daily meals can transform your health. For instance, turmeric contains curcumin, a compound with potent anti-inflammatory properties. Start incorporating these spices into your meals regularly, not just for their health benefits but for their ability to elevate the flavor of any dish.

Legumes and Beans: Protein-Packed and Fiber-Rich

Beans and legumes are excellent protein sources, essential for those reducing their intake of inflammatory meats. Chickpeas, lentils, and black beans are versatile and beneficial, rich in fiber and antioxidants, which help reduce inflammation and promote gut health.

Nuts and Seeds: Crunchy Allies

Almonds, chia seeds, flax seeds, and walnuts are not only delicious but are fantastic sources of anti-inflammatory fats, proteins, and fibers. They're perfect for snacks, as additions to salads, or even as part of a breakfast smoothie, making them versatile allies in your anti-inflammatory diet.

The Color Wheel of Fruits and Vegetables

Your pantry should also make room for the storage of particular fruits and vegetables that are staples for your diet. Items like sweet potatoes, beets, and all colors of bell peppers should have a place in your storage. These foods store well and provide a variety of nutrients and antioxidants that combat inflammation.

The Magic of Broths and Stocks

Imagine sipping a warm, flavorful broth that not only soothes the soul but also soothes inflammation. Stocks and broths made from bones, vegetables, and herbs simmered for hours are rich in minerals and vitamins and can serve as a base for numerous anti-inflammatory meals, from soups to grains.

Specialty Items: A Little Goes a Long Way

Certain specialty ingredients like matcha green tea, cocoa, and seaweed offer concentrated anti-inflammatory benefits. Adding just a bit of these to your pantry—and your diet—can contribute significantly to your health, proving that sometimes, a little really does go a long way.

Adapting to New Tastes and Textures

As you introduce new items into your pantry, give yourself time to adapt to different tastes and textures. Experiment with various preparation methods to find what pleases your palate while benefiting your body. Remember, every person's body reacts uniquely, so observe how your body responds and adjust your pantry staples accordingly.

Creating a Visually Appealing and Accessible Pantry

Organize your pantry in a way that makes these new, healthy choices the easiest ones. Place anti-inflammatory foods at eye level and in clear, easily accessible containers. Seeing these healthy options readily available will make choosing them feel more like second nature over time.

Continuous Learning and Experimentation

Embrace the process of learning as you go. Your pantry—and your diet—is not static; it should evolve as you gain more knowledge and experience with what foods best support your anti-inflammatory lifestyle. Always be open to trying new ingredients as they might just unlock new favorite dishes and health benefits.

By reimagining your pantry, you aren't just reorganizing a space in your home; you are setting the stage for a healthier life. Every item in your anti-inflammatory pantry serves a purpose, contributing to your daily wellness and vitality. With these staples at the ready, you can feel confident and empowered to sustain this healthful way of eating, enjoying every meal as part of your journey towards a more vibrant, energetic self.

MEAL PLANNING TIPS FOR BEGINNERS

Embarking on your anti-inflammatory journey with the ambition of transforming your dietary habits can be thrilling, yet daunting. A vital component for making this dietary shift is effective meal planning. Think of meal planning as drawing a map for your journey each week; it ensures you have all the necessary provisions and a clear route to maintain your new healthy eating habits.

Embracing the Concept of Batch Cooking

One of the cornerstone techniques in efficient meal planning is batch cooking. It's about cooking larger portions of certain meals or meal components once or twice a week so that you have a reliable stock of nutritious, homemade food ready to go. This could be anything from preparing a big pot of quinoa, roasting a tray of anti-inflammatory vegetables like sweet potatoes and brussels sprouts, or cooking a batch of bone broth. Having these ready can be a lifesaver on busy days when time or energy might deter you from cooking fresh.

Diversifying Your Meals

Variety isn't just the spice of life; it's also a fundamental aspect of a healthful diet. Eating a diverse range of foods ensures you get a broad spectrum of nutrients, vitamins, and minerals. When planning your meals, consider each food category in your anti-inflammatory diet and aim to include multiple sources of fats, proteins, and carbohydrates. This might mean having fish like salmon or mackerel, rich in Omega-3 fatty acids, a couple of times a week, alternating with plant-based protein sources such as lentils or beans.

Mapping Out Your Week

Each weekend, take some time to map out your meals for the week ahead. This isn't just about deciding what you'll eat and when; it's about anticipating the busy days and knowing you might need a quick-to-plate dish ready. Assign each meal a slot in your week, keeping flexibility in mind—some meals might need to be swapped around depending on how your week unfolds.

Shopping Smart

With your weekly meals mapped out, create a shopping list that aligns with these plans. Stick to this list when you go grocery shopping to avoid impulsive buys—especially those that don't align with your anti-inflammatory goals. Shopping from local farmers' markets can also be a fantastic way to get fresh, seasonal produce that supports your diet while also being environmentally and economically beneficial.

Utilizing Technology

In today's digital age, various apps and tools can assist with meal planning. Apps that help with recipe organization or even generate shopping lists based on your meal plan can cut down the time you spend planning and ensure you don't miss anything essential during your grocery runs.

The Freezer is Your Friend

Never underestimate the value of your freezer. It can be a great ally in your meal planning strategy. Freezing portions of meals, particularly soups and stews, can ensure you always have a healthy meal on hand when you're too tired or busy to cook. Labeling frozen items with contents and a date will help keep track of what's available and ensure food safety.

Lean on Leftovers

Transforming leftovers into new meals can be an art form that saves time and money and reduces waste. A roast chicken, for instance, can turn into chicken salad for lunch the next day or be added to a soup. Think of leftovers as a jumpstart to your next culinary creation, not just a repeat of last night's dinner.

Adjust as You Go

Flexibility is key in meal planning, as not everything always goes according to plan. You might find certain dishes aren't as filling as expected, or perhaps a recipe didn't turn out as you had hoped. Use these instances as learning opportunities to tweak your plan to better suit your needs. Eating should remain a joy, not a chore, so adjusting your meal plans to what delights and satisfies you is crucial.

Practice Makes Perfect

Like any new skill, effective meal planning gets easier with practice. Initially, you might find it a little challenging to get into the rhythm of thinking ahead, prepping, and cooking in batches. However, over time, as you begin to see the benefits—less stress around mealtime, better eating habits, more control over your diet—it becomes second nature.

Involve Your Household

If you're not eating alone, involve your household in the meal planning process. This can include deciding on meals together and even shopping or cooking together. It will not only make the process more enjoyable but also ensure that everyone's dietary needs and preferences are considered.

Enjoy the Process

Lastly, enjoy every step of this journey. From discovering new recipes that excite your taste buds to the moments spent chopping and sautéing, every phase adds to the rich tape rhythm of a healthy lifestyle. Celebrate your successes, learn from the missteps, and embrace the path to vibrant health through better eating habits.

Meal planning is not just a tool for dietary compliance; it's a vehicle that drives you towards a life of enriched health and everyday wellness. By adopting and refining these strategies, you'll not only foster a healthier relationship with food but also build a foundation that supports your anti-inflammatory lifestyle holistically.

CHAPTER 3: SMOOTHIES AND DRINKS

Imagine starting your day with a burst of anti-inflammatory goodness, a drink that not only tastes delightful but also infuses your body with everything it needs to combat inflammation and boost your energy levels. In this chapter, we explore the transformative power of smoothies and drinks, your secret weapon in the journey towards health and vitality.

Drinks, especially when infused with the right ingredients, can be powerful vessels of health. They work subtly, deliciously, and most importantly, they blend seamlessly into our busy lives. Whether it's a vibrant smoothie packed with berries and seeds or a soothing herbal tea, the right drink can set the tone for a nourishing day or serve as a replenishing pause in a hectic schedule.

Let me take you through the art and science of crafting beverages that do more than just quench your thirst. They soothe, heal, and energize. We'll delve into hydrating smoothies that employ fruits and vegetables known for their anti-inflammatory properties, such as dark leafy greens, tart cherries, and turmeric. Each sip is a step closer to reduced inflammation and enhanced well-being.

But it's not just about the what; it's about the how and the why. Understand why a certain combination of ingredients works better to lower inflammation and how you can maximize the benefits with simple tweaks. For instance, the addition of a pinch of black pepper to a turmeric drink can significantly boost the absorption of curcumin, the active ingredient in turmeric.

Through the recipes and insights shared here, you'll discover that making a drink isn't just a mundane routine; it's an alchemic process that transforms natural ingredients into elixirs of health. You will learn to create your concoctions, from immune-boosting drinks to energizing smoothies, each designed to fit effortlessly into your lifestyle and cater to your body's unique needs.

As you turn the pages, let each recipe be a brushstroke in the beautiful artwork of your healthful life. Embrace these drinks not just as part of your diet, but as a daily ritual of self-care and a celebration of health. Cheers to a vibrant, energized, and inflammation-free life!

ENERGIZING SMOOTHIES

GINGER TURMERIC SUNRISE SMOOTHIE

Preparation Time: 5 min
Cooking Time: none

Mode of Cooking: Blending
Servings: 2
Ingredients:

- 1 cup frozen mango chunks
- 1 small banana
- 1 cup coconut water
- 1/2 tsp turmeric powder
- 1/2 tsp freshly grated ginger
- 1 Tbsp chia seeds
- 1/2 tsp vanilla extract
- Juice of 1/2 lime

Directions:

1. Combine all ingredients in a blender and blend until smooth
2. Serve immediately in chilled glasses

Tips:

- Add a pinch of black pepper to enhance the absorption of turmeric
- Customize with a scoop of plant-based protein powder for an extra boost

Nutritional Values: Calories: 200, Fat: 2g, Carbs: 46g, Protein: 3g, Sugar: 32g

AVOCADO MATCHA ENERGY SHAKE

Preparation Time: 6 min
Cooking Time: none
Mode of Cooking: Blending
Servings: 1
Ingredients:

- 1 ripe avocado
- 1 cup spinach leaves
- 1/2 banana
- 1 cup almond milk
- 1 tsp matcha green tea powder
- 1 Tbsp honey
- 1/2 cup ice cubes
- 1 tsp lemon zest

Directions:

1. Place avocado, spinach, banana, almond milk, matcha powder, honey, ice cubes, and lemon zest into a blender
2. Blend on high until creamy and smooth
3. Pour into a glass and enjoy immediately

Tips:

- For a thinner consistency, add more almond milk
- Serve immediately for optimal freshness and flavor

Nutritional Values: Calories: 340, Fat: 21g, Carbs: 36g, Protein: 5g, Sugar: 20g

BLUEBERRY BASIL BOOSTER

Preparation Time: 7 min
Cooking Time: none
Mode of Cooking: Blending
Servings: 2
Ingredients:

- 1 cup blueberries, fresh or frozen
- 1 banana
- 1/2 cup Greek yogurt, unsweetened
- 1/4 cup fresh basil leaves
- 1 Tbsp flaxseed meal
- 1 cup coconut water
- 1 tsp lemon juice

Directions:

1. Combine blueberries, banana, yogurt, basil, flaxseed meal, coconut water, and lemon juice in a blender
2. Blend until smooth and well combined
3. Pour into glasses and serve chilled

Tips:

- Experiment with mint instead of basil for a different flavor profile
- Add a teaspoon of honey if more sweetness is desired

Nutritional Values: Calories: 190, Fat: 3g, Carbs: 35g, Protein: 6g, Sugar: 22g

CACAO BEET ENERGIZER

Preparation Time: 8 min
Cooking Time: none
Mode of Cooking: Blending
Servings: 2
Ingredients:

- 1/2 cup beetroot, cooked and peeled
- 1 cup strawberries, fresh or frozen
- 1 small banana
- 1 cup almond milk
- 2 Tbsp raw cacao powder
- 1 Tbsp almond butter

- 1 tsp vanilla extract
- 1/2 cup ice cubes

Directions:

1. Place beetroot, strawberries, banana, almond milk, cacao powder, almond>>();

Tips:

-

Nutritional Values:

PINEAPPLE COCONUT REVIVER

Preparation Time: 6 min
Cooking Time: none
Mode of Cooking: Blending
Servings: 2
Ingredients:

- 1 cup pineapple chunks, fresh or frozen
- 1/2 cup coconut meat
- 1 banana
- 1 cup coconut milk
- 1 Tbsp lime juice
- 1 tsp coconut extract
- 1/2 cup ice cubes

Directions:

2. Blend all ingredients together until creamy and smooth
3. Pour the smoothie into glasses and garnish with a slice of pineapple

Tips:

- Add a tablespoon of flaxseed for an omega-3 boost
- Freeze pineapple chunks ahead of time for an extra-frosty texture

Nutritional Values: Calories: 260, Fat: 12g, Carbs: 38g, Protein: 3g, Sugar: 25g

GOLDEN TURMERIC SUNRISE SMOOTHIE

Preparation Time: 5 min
Cooking Time: none
Mode of Cooking: Blending

Servings: 2
Ingredients:

- 1 cup coconut water
- 1 medium banana, frozen
- 1/2 cup mango chunks, frozen
- 1/4 cup carrots, chopped
- 1 Tbsp ground flaxseed
- 1/2 tsp turmeric powder
- 1/4 tsp ginger, grated
- 1 pinch black pepper
- 1 Tbsp honey

Directions:

1. Combine all ingredients in a blender and blend until smooth
2. Pour into glasses and serve immediately

Tips:

- Add a scoop of protein powder for an extra boost
- To enhance the anti-inflammatory effects, increase turmeric slightly, but be mindful of its strong flavor

Nutritional Values: Calories: 160, Fat: 1g, Carbs: 35g, Protein: 3g, Sugar: 22g

---

HYDRATING BEVERAGES

CUCUMBER MINT REFRESHER

Preparation Time: 5 min
Cooking Time: none
Mode of Cooking: Mixing
Servings: 2
Ingredients:

- 1 large cucumber, peeled and sliced
- 10 fresh mint leaves
- 1 Tbsp honey
- 2 Tbsp freshly squeezed lime juice
- 1 cup ice cubes
- 2 cups sparkling water

Directions:

1. Combine cucumber, mint leaves, honey, and lime juice in a blender and blend until smooth
2. Strain mixture into a pitcher, pressing solids to extract flavors
3. Add ice cubes and top with sparkling water, stir gently

Tips:

- Serve immediately with a sprig of mint for garnish
- You can sweeten it further with a bit of stevia if desired
- This drink can be made in advance and stored in the refrigerator for up to 24 hours

Nutritional Values: Calories: 50, Fat: 0.2g, Carbs: 12g, Protein: 0.6g, Sugar: 10g

GOLDEN PINEAPPLE TURMERIC TONIC

Preparation Time: 10 min
Cooking Time: none
Mode of Cooking: Blending
Servings: 2
Ingredients:

- 1 cup pineapple chunks
- 1-inch piece of turmeric root, peeled and chopped
- 1-inch piece of ginger root, peeled and chopped
- 1 Tbsp lemon juice
- 2 tsp raw honey
- 1 cup coconut water
- ½ tsp ground cinnamon
- pinch of black pepper

Directions:

1. Place all ingredients into a blender and blend on high until smooth
2. Strain the mixture using a fine mesh sieve into glasses

Tips:

- Add more honey if a sweeter taste is preferred
- Black pepper enhances the absorption of turmeric, do not omit it
- If you like a chilled beverage, use frozen pineapple chunks

Nutritional Values: Calories: 120, Fat: 0.5g, Carbs: 30g, Protein: 1g, Sugar: 20g

WATERMELON BASIL QUENCHER

Preparation Time: 7 min
Cooking Time: none
Mode of Cooking: Blending
Servings: 4
Ingredients:

- 4 cups cubed seedless watermelon
- ¼ cup fresh basil leaves
- 2 Tbsp lime juice
- 1 Tbsp chia seeds
- 4 cups chilled water

Directions:

1. Blend watermelon, basil leaves, and lime juice in a blender until smooth
2. Pour into a large pitcher and stir in chia seeds and chilled water
3. Let sit for 5 minutes to allow chia seeds to swell

Tips:

- Serve over ice for extra refreshment
- Basil can be swapped with mint for a different flavor profile
- This drink is rich in antioxidants and hydrating properties

Nutritional Values: Calories: 80, Fat: 1g, Carbs: 18g, Protein: 2g, Sugar: 15g

CHAMOMILE HONEYDEW COOLER

Preparation Time: 8 min
Cooking Time: none
Mode of Cooking: Blending
Servings: 2
Ingredients:

- 2 cups cubed honeydew melon
- 1 cup brewed chamomile tea, cooled
- 1 Tbsp raw honey
- 2 Tbsp lemon juice
- 1 cup ice cubes

Directions:

1. Blend all ingredients except ice until smooth in a blender
2. Add ice cubes and blend until frothy

Tips:

- Honey amount can be adjusted according to taste
- A sprig of mint or lavender can enhance the flavor and add a relaxing aroma
- Ideal as a pre-sleep beverage due to chamomile's soothing properties

Nutritional Values: Calories: 60, Fat: 0.3g, Carbs: 14g, Protein: 1g, Sugar: 12g

SPICY GINGER BEET ELIXIR

Preparation Time: 15 min
Cooking Time: none
Mode of Cooking: Juicing
Servings: 3
Ingredients:

- 2 medium beets, peeled and chopped
- 1 apple, cored and sliced
- 1-inch piece of ginger, peeled
- ½ lemon, peeled
- 1 pinch cayenne pepper
- 2 cups water

Directions:

1. Juice beets, apple, ginger, and lemon using a juicer
2. Mix the fresh juice with a pinch of cayenne pepper and water

Tips:

- If the flavor is too intense, adjust by adding more water
- Can be served warm for a soothing winter drink
- Rich in detoxifying properties and excellent for digestion

Nutritional Values: Calories: 90, Fat: 0.4g, Carbs: 22g, Protein: 2g, Sugar: 18g

GINGER PEACH ICED TEA

Preparation Time: 10 min
Cooking Time: 5 min
Mode of Cooking: Boiling
Servings: 4
Ingredients:

- 4 cups water
- 3 Tbsp loose black tea or 3 tea bags
- 1 inch ginger root, freshly grated
- 2 ripe peaches, pitted and sliced
- Honey or stevia to taste

Directions:

1. Boil water and steep tea with grated ginger for about 5 minutes
2. Remove tea bags or strain tea leaves
3. Add sliced peaches and sweetener to the tea and chill in the refrigerator
4. Serve cold with ice cubes

Tips:

- Serve this refreshing drink with a fresh peach slice on the rim of the glass for a decorative touch
- Ginger can be adjusted according to taste preference

Nutritional Values: Calories: 30, Fat: 0g, Carbs: 8g, Protein: 0g, Sugar: 7g

IMMUNE-BOOSTING DRINKS

GOLDEN TURMERIC TONIC

Preparation Time: 5 min
Cooking Time: none
Mode of Cooking: Mixing
Servings: 2
Ingredients:

- 1½ cups coconut water
- 1 tsp turmeric powder
- 1 Tbsp ginger, freshly grated
- 1 Tbsp honey
- Juice of 1 lemon
- Pinch of black pepper

Directions:

1. Combine all ingredients in a blender and blend until smooth
2. Pour into glasses and stir well before serving
3. Serve immediately or chill in the refrigerator for an enhanced flavor infusion

Tips:

- Add a cinnamon stick during blending for a spicy twist
- Use raw honey for additional antibacterial properties

Nutritional Values: Calories: 90, Fat: 0.5g, Carbs: 20g, Protein: 1g, Sugar: 12g

SPIRULINA SUNRISE SMOOTHIE

Preparation Time: 10 min
Cooking Time: none
Mode of Cooking: Blending
Servings: 1
Ingredients:

- 1 cup almond milk
- 1 ripe banana
- ½ cup frozen pineapple
- 1 Tbsp spirulina powder
- 1 tsp chia seeds
- 1 tsp flaxseed oil

Directions:

1. Add all ingredients into a high-speed blender
2. Blend until creamy and smooth
3. Taste and adjust sweetness, if necessary

Tips:

- Experiment with adding a handful of spinach for extra nutrients
- Store leftover smoothie in a sealed container in the fridge

Nutritional Values: Calories: 210, Fat: 4g, Carbs: 39g, Protein: 5g, Sugar: 20g

GINGER-LEMONGRASS TEA

Preparation Time: 15 min
Cooking Time: 10 min
Mode of Cooking: Simmering
Servings: 4
Ingredients:

- 4 cups water
- 2 inches ginger root, sliced
- 2 stalks lemongrass, cut into 2-inch pieces
- 1 Tbsp raw honey
- Juice of 1 lemon

Directions:

1. Bring water to a boil in a saucepan
2. Add ginger and lemongrass
3. Reduce heat and simmer for 10 min
4. Remove from heat and strain into mugs
5. Stir in honey and lemon juice

Tips:

- Serve with a slice of lemon for garnish
- Sweeten further if desired with additional honey

Nutritional Values: Calories: 40, Fat: 0g, Carbs: 10g, Protein: 0g, Sugar: 9g

MATCHA MINT REFRESHMENT

Preparation Time: 7 min
Cooking Time: none
Mode of Cooking: Mixing
Servings: 2
Ingredients:

- 1½ cups chilled green tea
- 1 tsp matcha powder
- Mint leaves, a handful
- Juice of ½ lime
- 1 tsp honey
- Ice cubes

Directions:

1. In a pitcher, whisk together matcha powder and a small amount of green tea to form a paste
2. Add the rest of the green tea, lime juice, honey, and mint leaves
3. Stir well until fully combined
4. Serve over ice

Tips:

- Experiment with adding a splash of coconut water for a tropical twist
- Press mint leaves with a muddler for more flavor release

Nutritional Values: Calories: 30, Fat: 0g, Carbs: 7g, Protein: 1g, Sugar: 4g

ANTIOXIDANT ACAI BOOSTER

Preparation Time: 8 min
Cooking Time: none
Mode of Cooking: Blending
Servings: 1
Ingredients:

- 1 frozen acai berry packet
- 1 cup pomegranate juice
- ½ banana
- 1 Tbsp ground flaxseed
- 1 tsp honey
- Ice cubes

Directions:

1. Blend acai berry packet, banana, pomegranate juice, flaxseed, and honey with ice cubes in a blender until smooth
2. Pour into a glass and garnish with a slice of banana
3. Serve immediately for best taste

Tips:

- Add a scoop of plant-based protein powder for a protein boost
- Garnish with fresh berries for an extra antioxidant kick

Nutritional Values: Calories: 180, Fat: 3g, Carbs: 35g, Protein: 3g, Sugar: 20g

GOLDEN TURMERIC TEA

Preparation Time: 5 min.
Cooking Time: 10 min.
Mode of Cooking: Simmering
Servings: 2
Ingredients:

- 2 cups water
- 1 inch fresh turmeric root, grated
- 1 inch fresh ginger root, grated
- 1 cinnamon stick
- 1 Tbsp honey
- Juice of half a lemon
- Pinch of black pepper

Directions:

1. Bring water to a gentle boil in a saucepan
2. Add turmeric, ginger, and cinnamon stick and simmer for 10 min.
3. Remove from heat and strain into mugs
4. Stir in honey, lemon juice, and black pepper

Tips:

- Drink warm and add a dash of cayenne pepper for extra heat if desired
- Store any leftovers in the refrigerator and enjoy within 24 hrs

Nutritional Values: Calories: 60, Fat: 0g, Carb: 16g, Protein: 0g, Sugar: 14g

CHAPTER 4: BREAKFASTS

Imagine greeting each morning not just with a cup of coffee, but with a plate that promises both nourishment and a nudge towards wellness. Breakfast, often hailed as the most important meal of the day, isn't just about quelling the morning hunger pangs—it's your first opportunity to combat inflammation and kickstart your day with vibrant energy.

In this chapter, we explore the wonders of anti-inflammatory breakfasts that do more than satiate: they soothe, strengthen, and support your body. The recipes and ideas contained here are designed to be as enjoyable as they are beneficial, making it simple to weave them into the fabric of your busy morning routine. Whether you're someone who spends their mornings scrambling to get out the door or you have the luxury of enjoying a languid start to the day, the diversity of recipes ensures there's an option just for you.

From hearty options that repair and fuel your body to light, refreshing choices that wake up your senses without weighing you down, each recipe is crafted with ingredients known for their anti-inflammatory properties. Picture beginning your day with a warm bowl of oatmeal infused with spices like turmeric and cinnamon, or a vibrant smoothie bowl adorned with a kaleidoscope of anti-oxidant-rich fruits. Not only are these meals a delight for the senses, but they also serve a crucial role in setting a positive tone for your day's eating habits.

What's more, embracing these breakfast ideas can transform your understanding of health. It's easy to fall prey to the convenience of processed foods, especially in the rush of the morning hours. But here, we lay down simple, fuss-free recipes that encourage even the busiest souls to pause and prioritize wellness. Each dish is a building block in your journey toward a comprehensive anti-inflammatory lifestyle, proving that each bite you take can be a step towards a healthier life.

So, let's break the overnight fast with choices that not only taste good but also do good. Ready your spoons and your spirits—because a beautiful morning awaits with every healthful bite.

HEARTY BREAKFASTS

TURMERIC QUINOA POWER BREAKFAST BOWL

Preparation Time: 15 min
Cooking Time: 20 min
Mode of Cooking: Stovetop
Servings: 2

Ingredients:

- 1 cup quinoa, rinsed
- 2 cups water
- 1 tsp turmeric powder
- 1 pinch black pepper
- 1 Tbsp coconut oil
- 1 large sweet potato, peeled and diced
- 1 avocado, thinly sliced
- 4 large kale leaves, de-stemmed and chopped
- 2 Tbsp pumpkin seeds
- 1 Tbsp flaxseeds
- 2 large eggs
- Salt to taste

Directions:

1. Rinse quinoa thoroughly and combine with water, turmeric, and black pepper in a saucepan, bring to a boil then simmer covered for 15 min until water is absorbed
2. Meanwhile, sauté sweet potatoes in coconut oil until tender, set aside
3. In the same pan, lightly sauté kale until slightly softened
4. Poach or fry eggs to desired doneness
5. Assemble bowl by dividing the quinoa, sweet potato, avocado, kale, and eggs between two bowls, sprinkle with pumpkin seeds and flaxseeds

Tips:

- Cook quinoa in a batch and use throughout the week for quick assembly
- Incorporate a drizzle of tahini for extra creaminess and flavor
- Adding a dash of chili flakes can enhance the flavor profile

Nutritional Values: Calories: 590, Fat: 22g, Carbs: 77g, Protein: 21g, Sugar: 5g

SAVORY OATMEAL WITH SHIITAKE MUSHROOMS AND SPINACH

Preparation Time: 10 min
Cooking Time: 15 min
Mode of Cooking: Stovetop
Servings: 2
Ingredients:

- 1 cup steel-cut oats
- 2 cups vegetable broth
- 1 cup shiitake mushrooms, sliced
- 1 cup fresh spinach, washed and torn
- 1 Tbsp olive oil
- 2 garlic cloves, minced
- 2 tsp soy sauce
- 1 tsp sesame oil
- Salt and pepper to taste
- 2 tsp chives, chopped for garnish

Directions:

1. Cook steel-cut oats in vegetable broth until tender and most of the broth is absorbed
2. In a separate pan, sauté garlic and mushrooms in olive oil until mushrooms are golden
3. Add spinach and cook until wilted
4. Stir in soy sauce and sesame oil
5. Combine the mushroom and spinach mixture with cooked oats, season with salt and pepper, garnish with chives

Tips:

- Use tamari instead of soy sauce for a gluten-free option
- Sauté additional vegetables like bell peppers or zucchini for more variety and increase in volume

Nutritional Values: Calories: 350, Fat: 14g, Carbs: 45g, Protein: 12g, Sugar: 2g

CHIA AND ALMOND OVERNIGHT OATS

Preparation Time: 10 min
Cooking Time: none
Mode of Cooking: No Cooking
Servings: 2
Ingredients:

- 1 cup rolled oats
- 2 Tbsp chia seeds
- 1 cup almond milk, unsweetened
- 1 medium banana, mashed
- 1/2 tsp cinnamon
- 2 Tbsp almond butter
- 1/4 cup almonds, chopped
- 2 Tbsp honey or maple syrup
- 1/4 tsp vanilla extract

Directions:

1. In a large bowl, mix oats, chia seeds, almond milk, mashed banana, cinnamon, almond butter, honey, and vanilla extract until well combined

2. Divide the mixture into jars or bowls, cover, and refrigerate overnight

3. In the morning, stir well and top with chopped almonds

Tips:

- Swap almond milk with coconut milk for a tropical twist
- Add fresh berries before serving for extra freshness and antioxidants
- Drizzle with additional honey or maple syrup for added sweetness if desired

Nutritional Values: Calories: 520, Fat: 16g, Carbs: 79g, Protein: 15g, Sugar: 20g

BROCCOLI AND CHICKPEA BREAKFAST HASH

Preparation Time: 15 min
Cooking Time: 20 min
Mode of Cooking: Stovetop
Servings: 3
Ingredients:

- 1 Tbsp olive oil
- 1 small onion, diced
- 2 cups broccoli florets
- 1 can (15 oz) chickpeas, drained and rinsed
- 1 red bell pepper, diced
- 1 tsp smoked paprika
- 1/2 tsp ground cumin
- Salt and black pepper to taste
- 3 large eggs

Directions:

1. Heat olive oil in a large skillet over medium heat, sauté onion until translucent

2. Add broccoli, chickpeas, and bell pepper, cook stirring occasionally until vegetables are tender

3. Stir in smoked paprika, cumin, salt, and pepper

4. Create three wells in the hash, crack an egg into each, cover and cook until eggs are set

Tips:

- Try adding a dollop of Greek yogurt on top for extra creaminess and a protein boost
- Garnish with fresh herbs like cilantro or parsley for added flavor and color
- For a vegan version, substitute eggs with tofu scramble

Nutritional Values: Calories: 435, Fat: 17g, Carbs: 53g, Protein: 22g, Sugar: 8g

MUSHROOM AND GOAT CHEESE FRITTATA

Preparation Time: 10 min
Cooking Time: 25 min
Mode of Cooking: Oven
Servings: 4
Ingredients:

- 6 large eggs
- 1/4 cup milk
- 1/2 cup goat cheese, crumbled
- 1 Tbsp olive oil
- 1 cup cremini mushrooms, sliced
- 1 small zucchini, sliced
- 1/4 cup sun-dried tomatoes, chopped
- Salt and pepper to taste
- 2 Tbsp fresh basil, chopped

Directions:

1. Preheat oven to 375°F (190°C)

2. Whisk eggs and milk together, stir in goat cheese, salt, and pepper

3. In an oven-safe skillet, sauté mushrooms and zucchini in olive oil until just tender

4. Add sun-dried tomatoes and pour egg mixture over the vegetables

5. Cook on stovetop until edges begin to set, then transfer to oven and bake until frittata is set, about 20 min

6. Garnish with fresh basil

Tips:

- Serve with a side salad for a complete meal

- Experiment with different types of cheese like feta or Swiss for varying flavors
- A dash of nutmeg can add a subtle depth to the egg mixture

Nutritional Values: Calories: 290, Fat: 21g, Carbs: 8g, Protein: 19g, Sugar: 4g

TURMERIC AND QUINOA POWER BREAKFAST BOWLS

Preparation Time: 15 min
Cooking Time: 25 min
Mode of Cooking: Stovetop
Servings: 2
Ingredients:

- 1 cup quinoa, rinsed
- 2 cups water
- 1 tsp turmeric powder
- 1 pinch black pepper
- 1 Tbsp olive oil
- 4 large eggs
- 1 avocado, sliced
- 1 handful arugula
- 4 radishes, thinly sliced
- 1 Tbsp pumpkin seeds, toasted
- Salt to taste

Directions:

1. Combine quinoa, water, turmeric, and black pepper in a medium saucepan and bring to a boil
2. Reduce heat to low, cover and simmer until quinoa is tender and water is absorbed, about 20 min
3. While quinoa cooks, heat olive oil in a skillet and fry eggs to desired doneness
4. Divide cooked quinoa into bowls, top each with a fried egg, avocado slices, arugula, radish slices, and sprinkle with pumpkin seeds

Tips:

- Serve with a squeeze of lemon for added zest

- Season with a dash of hot sauce for a spicy kick

Nutritional Values: Calories: 490, Fat: 22g, Carbs: 55g, Protein: 20g, Sugar: 3g

LIGHT BREAKFAST OPTIONS

CHIA AND COCONUT YOGURT PARFAIT

Preparation Time: 10 min
Cooking Time: none
Mode of Cooking: No Cooking
Servings: 2
Ingredients:

- 1 cup plain coconut yogurt
- 3 Tbsp chia seeds
- ½ cup mixed berries, fresh or frozen
- 2 Tbsp honey
- ¼ cup granola
- 1 Tbsp flaxseeds, ground

Directions:

1. Mix chia seeds with coconut yogurt and let sit for 5 minutes to thicken
2. Layer the thickened yogurt alternate with berries and granola in two serving glasses
3. Drizzle with honey and sprinkle ground flaxseeds on top

Tips:

- Switch out berries with seasonal fruits for variety
- Add nuts for extra crunch and protein
- Use agave syrup as a vegan alternative to honey

Nutritional Values: Calories: 295, Fat: 9g, Carbs: 44g, Protein: 8g, Sugar: 26g

SPINACH AND FETA BREAKFAST WRAPS

Preparation Time: 15 min
Cooking Time: 5 min
Mode of Cooking: Pan Frying

Servings: 4

Ingredients:

- 4 whole grain tortillas
- 1 cup baby spinach, fresh
- ½ cup feta cheese, crumbled
- 4 eggs, beaten
- 1 Tbsp olive oil
- ¼ tsp black pepper
- ¼ tsp salt

Directions:

1. Heat olive oil in a skillet over medium heat
2. Add beaten eggs and scramble till almost set
3. Stir in spinach and cook until wilted
4. Remove from heat and mix in feta cheese, salt, and pepper
5. Divide the mixture among tortillas, wrap tightly

Tips:

- Serve immediately for best taste
- Add sundried tomatoes for a tangy flavor boost
- Can be made ahead and stored in the refrigerator for a quick reheat

Nutritional Values: Calories: 225, Fat: 12g, Carbs: 20g, Protein: 12g, Sugar: 3g

APPLE CINNAMON QUINOA BOWL

Preparation Time: 10 min
Cooking Time: 15 min
Mode of Cooking: Simmering
Servings: 2
Ingredients:

- 1 cup quinoa, rinsed
- 2 cups water
- 1 tsp cinnamon
- 1 apple, chopped
- 2 Tbsp maple syrup
- ¼ cup walnuts, chopped
- 1 cup almond milk

Directions:

1. In a saucepan, bring water and quinoa to boil
2. Reduce heat to simmer, add cinnamon, and cook covered until quinoa is tender and water is absorbed, about 15 minutes
3. Stir in almond milk, chopped apple, and maple syrup
4. Heat through
5. Serve topped with chopped walnuts

Tips:

- Customize with different spices such as nutmeg or cardamom
- Use pear instead of apple for a different taste
- Top with a dollop of Greek yogurt for extra protein

Nutritional Values: Calories: 320, Fat: 8g, Carbs: 51g, Protein: 11g, Sugar: 12g

AVOCADO LIME SMOOTHIE

Preparation Time: 5 min
Cooking Time: none
Mode of Cooking: Blending
Servings: 2
Ingredients:

- 1 ripe avocado
- 1 cup spinach leaves
- 1 banana
- 2 Tbsp lime juice
- 1 cup unsweetened almond milk
- 1 Tbsp chia seeds
- 1 tsp honey

Directions:

1. Place all ingredients in a blender
2. Blend on high until smooth and creamy
3. Pour into glasses and serve immediately

Tips:

- Add a scoop of protein powder for extra nutrition

- Use coconut water in place of almond milk for a tropical twist
- Sweeten with stevia instead of honey if desired

Nutritional Values: Calories: 251, Fat: 14g, Carbs: 30g, Protein: 4g, Sugar: 13g

MUSHROOM AND HERB OMELET

Preparation Time: 10 min
Cooking Time: 10 min
Mode of Cooking: Frying
Servings: 1
Ingredients:

- 2 eggs, beaten
- ½ cup mushrooms, sliced
- 1 Tbsp chives, chopped
- 1 Tbsp parsley, chopped
- 2 Tbsp olive oil
- Salt and pepper to taste

Directions:

1. Heat 1 Tbsp olive oil in a non-stick frying pan
2. Sauté mushrooms until golden
3. Remove from pan and set aside
4. Add remaining oil to the pan
5. Pour in eggs, cook until they begin to set
6. Sprinkle herbs, mushrooms, salt, and pepper over eggs
7. Fold omelet in half and cook until set

Tips:

- Experiment with different herbs like tarragon or cilantro for a unique flavor
- Can be served with a slice of whole-grain toast for a fuller meal
- Top with a sprinkle of grated parmesan for added taste

Nutritional Values: Calories: 290, Fat: 23g, Carbs: 6g, Protein: 14g, Sugar: 2g

CHIA AND COCONUT YOGURT DELIGHT

Preparation Time: 10 min
Cooking Time: none
Mode of Cooking: No Cooking
Servings: 2
Ingredients:

- 1 cup unsweetened coconut yogurt
- 2 Tbsp chia seeds
- ½ cup fresh blueberries
- 1 Tbsp raw honey
- ¼ tsp ground cinnamon
- zest of 1 small lime

Directions:

1. Combine coconut yogurt and chia seeds in a bowl and let sit for 5 min to allow chia seeds to swell
2. Add blueberries, raw honey, ground cinnamon, and lime zest
3. Stir gently until all ingredients are well mixed

Tips:

- Serve immediately or let it chill in the refrigerator overnight for enhanced flavors
- Top with a few mint leaves for a refreshing twist
- Opt for raw, local honey to maximize health benefits

Nutritional Values: Calories: 280, Fat: 15g, Carbs: 35g, Protein: 6g, Sugar: 24g

QUICK BREAKFAST IDEAS

GREEN TEA CHIA PUDDING

Preparation Time: 10 min
Cooking Time: none
Mode of Cooking: No Cooking
Servings: 2
Ingredients:

- 1 cup unsweetened almond milk
- 3 Tbsp chia seeds

- 1 tsp matcha green tea powder
- 1 Tbsp honey
- ½ banana, sliced
- ¼ cup fresh raspberries

Directions:

1. Combine almond milk, chia seeds, and matcha powder in a jar and stir well
2. Add honey and mix until fully incorporated
3. Refrigerate overnight
4. Top with banana slices and raspberries before serving

Tips:

- Stir occasionally within the first hour to prevent clumping and ensure a smooth texture
- Personalize with a sprinkle of coconut flakes or a dollop of almond butter for extra flavor and nutrients

Nutritional Values: Calories: 295, Fat: 9g, Carbs: 45g, Protein: 8g, Sugar: 20g

SAVORY OAT HASH

Preparation Time: 15 min
Cooking Time: 5 min
Mode of Cooking: Pan Cooking
Servings: 1
Ingredients:

- ⅓ cup rolled oats
- ⅔ cup water
- 1 Tbsp olive oil
- 1 small onion, finely chopped
- ½ bell pepper, diced
- 1 clove garlic, minced
- ¼ tsp smoked paprika
- Salt and pepper to taste
- 1 large egg
- 2 Tbsp shredded cheddar cheese

Directions:

1. Bring water to boil in a small saucepan, add oats, reduce heat to low and cook until oats are tender, about 5 min
2. Heat olive oil in a skillet over medium heat
3. Add onion, bell pepper, and garlic, sauté until softened
4. Stir in cooked oats and paprika, season with salt and pepper
5. Create a well in the center, crack the egg into it, cook until egg is set
6. Sprinkle with cheddar before serving

Tips:

- Experiment with various herbs such as thyme or rosemary for a different flavor profile
- Serve alongside a slice of whole-grain toast for added fiber

Nutritional Values: Calories: 380, Fat: 21g, Carbs: 35g, Protein: 16g, Sugar: 4g

BERRY QUINOA BREAKFAST BOWL

Preparation Time: 10 min
Cooking Time: 20 min
Mode of Cooking: Boiling
Servings: 2
Ingredients:

- 1 cup quinoa, rinsed
- 2 cups water
- 1 Tbsp honey
- ½ tsp cinnamon
- ½ cup blueberries
- ½ cup sliced strawberries
- ¼ cup chopped almonds
- 1 tsp lemon zest

Directions:

1. In a saucepan, bring quinoa and water to a boil, cover, and reduce to simmer for 15 min or until water is absorbed

2. Remove from heat, let stand covered for 5 min
3. Fluff quinoa with a fork, then stir in honey and cinnamon
4. Transfer to bowls, top with blueberries, strawberries, almonds, and lemon zest

Tips:

- Substitute honey with agave nectar if preferred for a vegan option
- Top with a dollop of Greek yogurt for added creaminess and protein

Nutritional Values: Calories: 320, Fat: 8g, Carbs: 53g, Protein: 11g, Sugar: 14g

SPINACH AND FETA BREAKFAST WRAP

Preparation Time: 10 min
Cooking Time: 5 min
Mode of Cooking: Pan Cooking
Servings: 1
Ingredients:

- 1 whole wheat tortilla
- 1 tsp olive oil
- 1 cup fresh spinach
- 2 egg whites
- 1 oz feta cheese, crumbled
- 1 Tbsp diced sun-dried tomatoes
- Salt and pepper to taste

Directions:

1. Heat olive oil in a skillet over medium heat
2. Add spinach and cook until wilted
3. In a bowl, whisk egg whites and pour over spinach, cooking until set
4. Sprinkle feta and sun-dried tomatoes on top, season with salt and pepper
5. Scoop onto tortilla, roll up to serve

Tips:

- Experiment with different leafy greens like kale or Swiss chard
- Add a few slices of avocado for a boost of healthy fats and creaminess

Nutritional Values: Calories: 280, Fat: 15g, Carbs: 27g, Protein: 20g, Sugar: 3g

ALMOND BUTTER AND BANANA OPEN SANDWICH

Preparation Time: 5 min
Cooking Time: none
Mode of Cooking: No Cooking
Servings: 1
Ingredients:

- 1 slice of whole-grain bread, toasted
- 2 Tbsp almond butter
- 1 banana, sliced
- 1 tsp chia seeds
- 1 tsp honey

Directions:

1. Spread almond butter on toasted bread
2. Arrange banana slices over almond butter
3. Sprinkle chia seeds and drizzle honey on top
4. Serve immediately

Tips:

- For a crunchier texture, add a handful of granola
- Drizzle with dark chocolate for a decadent touch
- Warm honey before drizzling to enhance its flavor and make spreading easier

Nutritional Values: Calories: 410, Fat: 18g, Carbs: 52g, Protein: 12g, Sugar: 24g

CHIA & COCONUT BREAKFAST PUDDING

Preparation Time: 10 min
Cooking Time: none
Mode of Cooking: No Cooking
Servings: 2
Ingredients:

- 1/3 C. chia seeds
- 1 C. light coconut milk
- 2 tsp. raw honey
- 1/2 tsp. vanilla extract

- 1/4 tsp. ground cinnamon
- 1/2 C. fresh berries
- 2 Tbsp shredded coconut, unsweetened

Directions:

1. Combine chia seeds, coconut milk, honey, vanilla extract, and cinnamon in a bowl and stir thoroughly

2. Allow the mixture to sit for at least 10 minutes until the chia seeds have absorbed the liquid and the mixture has thickened

3. Top with fresh berries and shredded coconut before serving

Tips:

- Best served chilled for enhanced flavor and texture
- Customize with different berries or fruits according to season for a varied flavor profile

Nutritional Values: Calories: 295, Fat: 19g, Carbs: 25g, Protein: 6g, Sugar: 12g

CHAPTER 5: SALADS

Imagine a canvas, vibrant and vivid, where each stroke adds life, color, and nutrition to not just a plate, but your overall wellbeing. That's what we embark upon in this chapter on salads. Far from the mundane tossed greens, the anti-inflammatory salads we explore here are hearty, filled with texture, and brimming with flavors that dance on the palate, while serving as powerful allies in your journey toward a healthier life.

Salads are the embodiment of versatility in your diet. Each recipe curated in this chapter is a testament to the fact that healthy eating doesn't require a compromise on taste or satisfaction. Think of a bowl filled with crisp spinach, sprinkled with vibrant pomegranate seeds, crunchy walnuts, and drizzled with a ginger-turmeric dressing. Not only does this salad awaken your senses, but it also calms your body's inflammatory responses, thanks to the powerhouse of nutrients packed in each ingredient.

Navigating through this array of salads, you'll discover combinations that might surprise you. From the protein-rich quinoa and black bean salad to a refreshing mix of zucchini and mint, these dishes are designed to provide essential nutrients that fight inflammation, bolster your energy levels, and revitalize your body. Each bite is a step further in your wellness journey, reinforcing the connection between a well-fed body and a vibrant, energetic life.

In this chapter, the simple act of preparing a salad becomes a delightful culinary adventure—an opportunity to mix ingredients that not only taste good together but also work together to heal and rejuvenate your body. Whether it's a quick lunch or a festive family dinner, these salads are crafted to suit any occasion, proving that your path to better health can be as enjoyable as it is nourishing. Let these recipes be your guide and your inspiration, reminding you that every meal is a chance to feed your body, mind, and soul with the goodness of nature.

REFRESHING SALADS

WATERMELON AND FETA SALAD WITH MINT

Preparation Time: 15 min.
Cooking Time: none
Mode of Cooking: No Cooking
Servings: 4

Ingredients:

- 4 cups watermelon, cubed
- 1 cup feta cheese, crumbled
- ½ cup fresh mint leaves, finely chopped
- 2 Tbsp extra virgin olive oil
- 1 Tbsp balsamic vinegar
- ¼ tsp freshly ground black pepper
- ⅛ tsp pink Himalayan salt

Directions:

1. Combine watermelon, crumbled feta, and chopped mint in a large bowl
2. Drizzle with olive oil and balsamic vinegar
3. Season with black pepper and Himalayan salt
4. Gently toss to combine

Tips:

- To enhance flavors, allow the salad to chill for about 30 minutes before serving
- Pair with a chilled glass of rosé for a summer feast

Nutritional Values: Calories: 180, Fat: 12g, Carbs: 15g, Protein: 5g, Sugar: 12g

AVOCADO AND MANGO SALAD WITH CITRUS DRESSING

Preparation Time: 20 min.
Cooking Time: none
Mode of Cooking: No Cooking
Servings: 4
Ingredients:

- 2 ripe avocados, peeled and diced
- 1 large ripe mango, peeled and diced
- 1 medium red onion, thinly sliced
- ¼ cup cilantro, chopped
- Dressing: 2 Tbsp orange juice
- 1 Tbsp lemon juice
- 2 Tbsp extra virgin olive oil
- 1 tsp honey
- ¼ tsp salt
- ⅛ tsp ground black pepper

Directions:

1. In a small bowl, whisk together orange juice, lemon juice, olive oil, honey, salt, and pepper to make the dressing
2. In a larger bowl, combine avocados, mango, red onion, and cilantro
3. Pour the dressing over the salad and toss gently to combine

Tips:

- Serve immediately to prevent avocados from browning
- This salad pairs beautifully with grilled seafood or chicken for a nutritious meal

Nutritional Values: Calories: 240, Fat: 15g, Carbs: 28g, Protein: 3g, Sugar: 20g

ASIAN CUCUMBER AND EDAMAME SALAD WITH WASABI VINAIGRETTE

Preparation Time: 15 min.
Cooking Time: none
Mode of Cooking: No Cooking
Servings: 4
Ingredients:

- 2 large cucumbers, spiralized or thinly sliced
- 1 cup edamame, shelled and cooked
- 1 small red bell pepper, thinly sliced
- 2 green onions, chopped
- 1 Tbsp sesame seeds
- Dressing: 2 Tbsp rice vinegar
- 1 Tbsp soy sauce
- 1 tsp wasabi paste
- 1 tsp grated ginger
- 2 Tbsp sesame oil

Directions:

1. Combine all vegetables and sesame seeds in a large bowl
2. In a separate bowl, mix together rice vinegar, soy sauce, wasabi paste, grated ginger, and sesame oil to create the dressing
3. Pour the dressing over the salad and toss well

Tips:

- The sharpness of wasabi in the dressing brings a delightful kick to this refreshing salad
- This dish can be stored in the refrigerator for up to 24 hours, making it a great make-ahead option for busy days

Nutritional Values: Calories: 130, Fat: 9g, Carbs: 9g, Protein: 5g, Sugar: 4g

ARTICHOKE AND ROASTED RED PEPPER SALAD

Preparation Time: 10 min.
Cooking Time: none
Mode of Cooking: No Cooking
Servings: 4

Ingredients:

- 1 can (14 oz.) artichoke hearts, drained and chopped
- 1 cup roasted red peppers, chopped
- ¼ cup Kalamata olives, pitted and sliced
- ¼ cup flat-leaf parsley, chopped
- Dressing: 3 Tbsp extra virgin olive oil
- 1 Tbsp white wine vinegar
- 1 tsp Dijon mustard
- Salt and black pepper to taste

Directions:

1. Mix artichoke hearts, roasted red peppers, Kalamata olives, and parsley in a large bowl
2. Whisk together olive oil, white wine vinegar, Dijon mustard, salt, and black pepper to make the dressing
3. Drizzle dressing over the salad and toss to coat evenly

Tips:

- This salad's robust flavors develop more fully if allowed to sit for about an hour before serving
- Try adding a sprinkle of crumbled feta or shaved Parmesan for a richer flavor profile

Nutritional Values: Calories: 150, Fat: 12g, Carbs: 9g, Protein: 2g, Sugar: 2g

CRISPY KALE AND QUINOA SALAD WITH FRESH APPLE SLICES

Preparation Time: 15 min
Cooking Time: none
Mode of Cooking: No Cooking
Servings: 4
Ingredients:

- 1 bunch kale, stems removed and leaves finely chopped
- 1 cup quinoa, cooked and cooled
- 1 large apple, cored and thinly sliced
- 1/4 cup dried cranberries
- 1/4 cup pumpkin seeds, toasted

- 3 Tbsp extra virgin olive oil
- 2 Tbsp apple cider vinegar
- 1 Tbsp honey
- 1 tsp Dijon mustard
- Salt and pepper to taste

Directions:

1. Massage kale with olive oil and a pinch of salt until leaves are tender and slightly wilted
2. In a large mixing bowl, add massaged kale, quinoa, apple slices, dried cranberries, and toasted pumpkin seeds
3. In a separate bowl, whisk together apple cider vinegar, honey, Dijon mustard, and a pinch of salt and pepper to create the dressing
4. Pour dressing over salad and toss to combine thoroughly

Tips:

- Tip: Let the salad sit for 10 minutes before serving to allow flavors to meld
- Add goat cheese or feta for a creamy texture and tangy flavor

Nutritional Values: Calories: 295, Fat: 14g, Carbs: 39g, Protein: 7g, Sugar: 14g

WATERMELON AND FETA SALAD WITH MINT DRIZZLE

Preparation Time: 10 min
Cooking Time: none
Mode of Cooking: No Cooking
Servings: 4
Ingredients:

- 2 cups watermelon, cut into cubes
- 1 cup arugula
- 1/2 cup feta cheese, crumbled
- 1/4 cup mint leaves, finely chopped
- 1/4 cup pistachios, chopped
- 2 Tbsp balsamic reduction
- 1 Tbsp olive oil
- 1/2 tsp black pepper
- 1/4 tsp salt

Directions:

1. In a large salad bowl, combine watermelon cubes, arugula, crumbled feta cheese, and chopped pistachios

2. In a small bowl, mix chopped mint leaves, olive oil, balsamic reduction, salt, and pepper to create the mint drizzle

3. Gently toss the salad with the mint drizzle just before serving

Tips:

- Tip: Chill the watermelon cubes before assembling the salad to enhance freshness and flavor

- Serve this salad as a refreshing starter to a summer meal

Nutritional Values: Calories: 180, Fat: 9g, Carbs: 20g, Protein: 5g, Sugar: 14g

PROTEIN-PACKED SALADS

QUINOA AND BLACK BEAN SALAD WITH CILANTRO-LIME DRESSING

Preparation Time: 15 min
Cooking Time: none
Mode of Cooking: No Cooking
Servings: 4
Ingredients:

- 1 cup quinoa, cooked and cooled
- 1 can black beans, drained and rinsed
- 1 red bell pepper, diced
- 1 cup frozen corn, thawed
- ½ red onion, finely chopped
- 1 cup cherry tomatoes, halved
- ¼ cup cilantro, chopped
- Juice of 2 limes
- 1 Tbsp olive oil
- Salt and pepper to taste

Directions:

1. Combine quinoa, black beans, bell pepper, corn, onion, and cherry tomatoes in a large bowl

2. In a small bowl, whisk together cilantro, lime juice, olive oil, salt, and pepper

3. Pour dressing over the salad and toss to coat evenly

Tips:

- Add avocado slices before serving for extra creaminess and a boost of healthy fats

- Chill the salad for at least an hour before serving to enhance the flavors

Nutritional Values: Calories: 320, Fat: 8g, Carbs: 52g, Protein: 12g, Sugar: 5g

SMOKED TURKEY AND SPINACH SALAD WITH CRANBERRY VINAIGRETTE

Preparation Time: 20 min
Cooking Time: none
Mode of Cooking: No Cooking
Servings: 4
Ingredients:

- 2 cups baby spinach
- 1 cup smoked turkey breast, sliced
- ½ cup dried cranberries
- ½ cup walnuts, toasted
- 1/4 cup goat cheese, crumbled
- 3 Tbsp extra virgin olive oil
- 2 Tbsp cranberry juice
- 1 Tbsp balsamic vinegar
- 1 tsp honey
- Salt and pepper to taste

Directions:

1. Arrange spinach on a platter and top with turkey, cranberries, walnuts, and goat cheese

2. In a jar, combine olive oil, cranberry juice, balsamic vinegar, honey, salt, and pepper; shake well to emulsify

3. Drizzle the vinaigrette over the salad just before serving

Tips:

- Serve immediately after dressing to prevent the spinach from wilting
- Pair with a crisp white wine for a refreshing meal

Nutritional Values: Calories: 290, Fat: 20g, Carbs: 18g, Protein: 14g, Sugar: 14g

GRILLED CHICKEN AND QUINOA TABBOULEH SALAD

Preparation Time: 30 min
Cooking Time: 10 min
Mode of Cooking: Grilling
Servings: 4
Ingredients:

- 1 cup quinoa, cooked and cooled
- 2 chicken breasts, grilled and sliced
- 1 cucumber, diced
- 2 tomatoes, diced
- ½ cup parsley, chopped
- ¼ cup mint, chopped
- 3 Tbsp lemon juice
- 2 Tbsp olive oil
- Salt and pepper to taste

Directions:

1. Mix cooked quinoa, cucumber, tomatoes, parsley, and mint in a large bowl
2. Whisk together lemon juice, olive oil, salt, and pepper in a small bowl to create the dressing
3. Add the grilled chicken to the salad and pour the dressing over, tossing well to combine

Tips:

- Marinate the chicken in lemon juice and olive oil before grilling for extra flavor
- Serve chill to let the flavors meld together

Nutritional Values: Calories: 365, Fat: 14g, Carbs: 34g, Protein: 26g, Sugar: 4g

ASIAN TOFU SALAD WITH SESAME GINGER DRESSING

Preparation Time: 25 min
Cooking Time: none
Mode of Cooking: No Cooking
Servings: 4
Ingredients:

- 2 cups mixed greens
- 1 block firm tofu, drained and cubed
- 1 carrot, julienned
- 1 red bell pepper, julienned
- 1 cup edamame, shelled and cooked
- 2 Tbsp sesame seeds
- 3 Tbsp soy sauce
- 2 Tbsp rice vinegar
- 1 Tbsp sesame oil
- 1 Tbsp ginger, minced
- 1 garlic clove, minced
- 1 tsp honey

Directions:

1. Toss mixed greens, tofu, carrot, bell pepper, and edamame in a large salad bowl
2. In a small bowl, combine soy sauce, rice vinegar, sesame oil, ginger, garlic, and honey to make the dressing
3. Pour dressing over the salad and sprinkle with sesame seeds before serving

Tips:

- For a spicy kick, add a dash of sriracha to the dressing
- Gently press tofu between paper towels to remove excess moisture before adding to the salad

Nutritional Values: Calories: 210, Fat: 12g, Carbs: 14g, Protein: 13g, Sugar: 3g

CHICKPEA AND ROASTED VEGETABLE SALAD WITH CUMIN VINAIGRETTE

Preparation Time: 40 min
Cooking Time: 30 min
Mode of Cooking: Roasting
Servings: 4
Ingredients:

- 2 cups chickpeas, rinsed and drained
- 1 zucchini, sliced and quartered
- 1 red onion, sliced
- 1 red bell pepper, sliced
- 1 yellow bell pepper, sliced
- 3 Tbsp olive oil
- 2 tsp ground cumin
- 3 Tbsp red wine vinegar
- 1 tsp honey
- Salt and pepper to taste

Directions:

1. Toss zucchini, red onion, and bell peppers with 2 Tbsp olive oil, salt, and pepper; roast at 425°F (220°C) for 30 min
2. Whisk together 1 Tbsp olive oil, cumin, red wine vinegar, honey, salt, and pepper to create the dressing
3. Combine roasted vegetables, chickpeas, and dressing in a salad bowl and mix well

Tips:

- Roast vegetables until they are caramelized to enhance their natural sweetness
- Allow the salad to sit for 10 minutes after mixing to let the flavors mix thoroughly

Nutritional Values: Calories: 275, Fat: 10g, Carbs: 39g, Protein: 9g, Sugar: 11g

CHICKPEA TUNA SALAD WITH AVOCADO DRESSING

Preparation Time: 15 min
Cooking Time: none
Mode of Cooking: No Cooking
Servings: 4

Ingredients:

- 2 cans chickpeas, rinsed and drained
- 2 cans albacore tuna in water, drained
- 1 large cucumber, diced
- 1 red bell pepper, diced
- 1 cup cherry tomatoes, halved
- 1 small red onion, thinly sliced
- 1 ripe avocado
- 2 Tbsp lemon juice
- 1 clove garlic, minced
- 2 Tbsp extra virgin olive oil
- Salt and black pepper to taste

Directions:

1. Mash avocado with lemon juice, garlic, olive oil, salt, and black pepper to create the dressing
2. In a large bowl, combine chickpeas, tuna, cucumber, bell pepper, cherry tomatoes, and red onion
3. Pour the avocado dressing over the salad and toss gently until well coated

Tips:

- Consider chilling the salad for 30 min before serving for enhanced flavor fusion
- Add a splash of apple cider vinegar to the dressing for a tangier taste

Nutritional Values: Calories: 310, Fat: 9g, Carbs: 30g, Protein: 27g, Sugar: 5g

---

CREATIVE SALAD COMBINATIONS

ROASTED BEET AND CITRUS SALAD WITH PISTACHIO DRESSING

Preparation Time: 15 min.
Cooking Time: none
Mode of Cooking: No Cooking
Servings: 4
Ingredients:

- 3 medium beets, roasted and sliced

- 2 oranges, peeled and segments
- 1 grapefruit, peeled and segments
- 2 cups arugula
- ¼ cup shelled pistachios, chopped
- 3 Tbsp extra virgin olive oil
- 1 Tbsp apple cider vinegar
- 1 tsp honey
- Salt and pepper to taste

Directions:

1. Wash and roast beets until tender, then slice
2. Segment oranges and grapefruit, ensuring to remove all the pith
3. Combine arugula, beet slices, orange and grapefruit segments in a large salad bowl
4. In a separate small bowl, mix olive oil, apple cider vinegar, honey, salt, and pepper to create the dressing
5. Drizzle dressing over the salad and toss gently to coat
6. Garnish with chopped pistachios

Tips:

- Add goat cheese for a creamy texture
- Serve immediately or keep chilled in the fridge until serving for enhanced flavor integration

Nutritional Values: Calories: 200, Fat: 10g, Carbs: 24g, Protein: 4g, Sugar: 16g

AVOCADO AND STRAWBERRY QUINOA SALAD

Preparation Time: 20 min.
Cooking Time: 15 min.
Mode of Cooking: Boiling
Servings: 6
Ingredients:

- 1 cup quinoa
- 2 cups water
- 1 avocado, diced
- 1 cup strawberries, sliced
- ½ cup cucumber, diced
- ¼ cup red onion, finely chopped

- ¼ cup fresh mint, chopped
- 2 Tbsp balsamic vinegar
- 3 Tbsp olive oil
- Salt and pepper to taste

Directions:

1. Rinse quinoa thoroughly under cold water
2. Boil water and add quinoa, reduce heat and simmer covered until water is absorbed and quinoa is fluffy, about 15 min.
3. Allow quinoa to cool
4. In a large mixing bowl, combine cooled quinoa with diced avocado, sliced strawberries, diced cucumber, chopped red onion, and chopped mint
5. In a small bowl, whisk together balsamic vinegar and olive oil, season with salt and pepper
6. Pour dressing over salad and toss to combine

Tips:

- Chill the salad for at least an hour before serving to enhance the flavors
- Top with feta cheese if desired for added richness

Nutritional Values: Calories: 210, Fat: 11g, Carbs: 26g, Protein: 4g, Sugar: 5g

SPICY WATERMELON AND CUCUMBER SALAD

Preparation Time: 10 min.
Cooking Time: none
Mode of Cooking: No Cooking
Servings: 4
Ingredients:

- 2 cups watermelon, cubed
- 1 large cucumber, sliced
- 1 jalapeno, thinly sliced
- ¼ cup lime juice
- 2 Tbsp honey
- ¼ tsp salt
- 1/8 tsp black pepper
- ½ cup fresh cilantro, roughly chopped

- ¼ cup feta cheese, crumbled

Directions:

1. Combine watermelon, cucumber, and jalapeno in a large bowl
2. In a small bowl, create a dressing by whisking together lime juice, honey, salt, and black pepper
3. Pour dressing over the watermelon mixture and toss gently
4. Garnish with chopped cilantro and crumbled feta cheese before serving

Tips:

- Serve chilled for a refreshing taste
- Adjust the amount of jalapeno according to your spice preference
- Add a pinch of chili powder for extra spice if desired

Nutritional Values: Calories: 120, Fat: 2g, Carbs: 24g, Protein: 2g, Sugar: 20g

CHARRED CORN AND MANGO SALAD

Preparation Time: 15 min.
Cooking Time: 10 min.
Mode of Cooking: Grilling
Servings: 6
Ingredients:

- 4 ears of corn, husks removed
- 1 ripe mango, peeled and diced
- 1 red bell pepper, diced
- ½ red onion, finely chopped
- 1 jalapeno, deseeded and minced
- Juice of 1 lime
- 3 Tbsp olive oil
- 1 Tbsp honey
- ¼ cup fresh coriander, chopped
- Salt and pepper to taste

Directions:

1. Grill corn over medium heat until charred on all sides, then remove from heat and let cool
2. Slice kernels off the cob and place in a large mixing bowl
3. Add diced mango, bell pepper, onion, and jalapeno to the bowl
4. In a smaller bowl, mix lime juice, olive oil, honey, salt, and pepper to create the dressing
5. Pour dressing over the corn mixture and toss to evenly coat
6. Garnish with chopped coriander before serving

Tips:

- Can be served warm or at room temperature
- Add roasted peanuts for a crunchy texture
- Drizzle with a bit more lime juice just before serving for extra zest

Nutritional Values: Calories: 180, Fat: 7g, Carbs: 28g, Protein: 3g, Sugar: 13g

ASIAN PEAR AND BABY SPINACH SALAD WITH GORGONZOLA

Preparation Time: 10 min.
Cooking Time: none
Mode of Cooking: No Cooking
Servings: 4
Ingredients:

- 2 Asian pears, cored and thinly sliced
- 4 cups baby spinach
- ½ cup gorgonzola cheese, crumbled
- ¼ cup dried cranberries
- ¼ cup walnuts, toasted and chopped
- 3 Tbsp balsamic vinegar
- 2 Tbsp extra virgin olive oil
- 1 tsp honey
- Salt and pepper to taste

Directions:

1. In a large salad bowl, combine sliced Asian pears, baby spinach, crumbled gorgonzola, dried cranberries, and toasted walnuts
2. In a small bowl, whisk together balsamic vinegar, olive oil, honey, salt, and pepper

3. Drizzle dressing over the salad and toss gently to combine

Tips:

- Serve immediately to prevent pears from browning
- Pair with a crisp white wine for a delightful meal
- Toast walnuts slightly before adding to the salad to enhance their flavor

Nutritional Values: Calories: 220, Fat: 15g, Carbs: 20g, Protein: 5g, Sugar: 14g

RAINBOW QUINOA AND POMEGRANATE SALAD

Preparation Time: 20 min
Cooking Time: none
Mode of Cooking: No Cooking
Servings: 4
Ingredients:

- 1 C. quinoa, cooked and cooled
- 1/2 C. pomegranate seeds
- 1 medium avocado, diced
- 1/2 C. cucumber, diced
- 1/4 C. red onion, finely chopped
- 1/4 C. fresh cilantro, chopped
- 2 Tbsp extra virgin olive oil
- Juice of 1 lime
- 1/4 tsp salt
- 1/4 tsp black pepper

Directions:

1. Combine quinoa, pomegranate seeds, avocado, cucumber, red onion, and cilantro in a large bowl
2. In a small bowl, whisk together olive oil, lime juice, salt, and pepper to create a dressing
3. Drizzle the dressing over the salad and toss gently to coat

Tips:

- Serve immediately for the freshest taste or chill for 30 minutes for flavors to meld more deeply
- Garnish with additional cilantro leaves if desired

Nutritional Values: Calories: 248, Fat: 15g, Carbs: 27g, Protein: 5g, Sugar: 5g

CHAPTER 6: SOUPS

Imagine this: a chilly evening, a cozy blanket, and a bowl of soup that not only warms your body but also bathes your cells in anti-inflammatory goodness. Soups have this magical way of healing and comforting us, don't they? In this chapter, we will dive into the world of nourishing soups, each recipe crafted not only to satisfy your taste buds but also to aid your body in its fight against inflammation.

Soup, in its humble essence, is a healer. It's your best ally on days when you feel down, and it's a powerful tool in your wellness arsenal, designed to help reduce inflammation caused by stress, environmental factors, and less-than-ideal eating habits. By incorporating ingredients known for their anti-inflammatory properties—think turmeric, ginger, garlic, and a bounty of fresh vegetables—we transform a simple meal into a therapeutic experience.

But why soups? The beauty of soups lies in their versatility and ease of preparation. Whether it's a creamy butternut squash soup for a touch of comfort or a robust lentil soup packed with protein and fiber, each spoonful helps soothe inflammation and nurture your body. Soups also allow the flavors of various anti-inflammatory foods to meld together beautifully, enhancing their natural flavors and maximizing their health benefits.

In this chapter, we will explore a range of soup recipes—from the nourishing broths that form the base of so many cultures' cuisines to creamy soups that feel like a warm hug from the inside out. We'll also examine how to extract the most health benefits from your ingredients, ensuring that every sip offers both comfort and healing.

So, grab your pot and ready your spoon as we prepare to simmer our way to better health. These recipes are designed to make your culinary journey enjoyable and your path to wellness as smooth as the velvety soups you'll soon be creating. Here's to warming both heart and health, one bowl at a time!

NOURISHING SOUPS

GOLDEN TURMERIC CHICKEN SOUP

Preparation Time: 15 min
Cooking Time: 25 min
Mode of Cooking: Stovetop
Servings: 4

Ingredients:

- 1 lb. chicken breast, diced
- 2 Tbsp coconut oil
- 1 large onion, chopped
- 3 cloves garlic, minced
- 2 tsp ground turmeric
- 1 tsp ground ginger
- 6 cups low-sodium chicken broth
- 1 cup coconut milk
- 2 carrots, sliced
- 2 stalks celery, sliced
- Salt and pepper to taste
- Fresh cilantro for garnish

Directions:

1. Heat coconut oil in a large pot over medium-high heat
2. Add onion and cook until translucent
3. Add garlic, turmeric, and ginger, stirring for about 1 min
4. Add diced chicken, cooking until lightly browned
5. Pour in chicken broth and bring to a boil
6. Reduce heat to simmer, adding carrots and celery, cook until vegetables are tender, about 15 min
7. Stir in coconut milk and season with salt and pepper
8. Simmer for an additional 5 min
9. Serve hot, garnished with fresh cilantro

Tips:

- Use homemade broth for deeper flavor and reduced sodium
- Incorporate a squeeze of lime juice for a tangy twist
- Serve with a side of jasmine rice for a filling meal

Nutritional Values: Calories: 310, Fat: 18g, Carbs: 9g, Protein: 28g, Sugar: 3g

ROASTED RED PEPPER AND TOMATO BISQUE

Preparation Time: 10 min
Cooking Time: 30 min
Mode of Cooking: Stovetop
Servings: 6
Ingredients:

- 3 cups roasted red peppers, chopped
- 4 tomatoes, peeled and diced
- 2 Tbsp extra-virgin olive oil
- 1 onion, diced
- 3 cloves garlic, minced
- 4 cups vegetable broth
- 1 tsp smoked paprika
- 1/2 tsp crushed red pepper flakes
- 1/2 cup heavy cream
- Salt and pepper to taste
- Fresh basil for garnish

Directions:

1. Heat olive oil in a large saucepan over medium heat
2. Add onions, cook until soft
3. Stir in garlic, smoked paprika, and red pepper flakes, cooking for 1 min
4. Add chopped tomatoes and roasted red peppers, cook for another 5 min
5. Pour in vegetable broth, bring to a boil, then reduce heat to simmer for 20 min
6. Puree the soup in batches in a blender until smooth
7. Return to pot, stir in heavy cream, season with salt and pepper
8. Heat through
9. Serve garnished with fresh basil

Tips:

- Opt for fire-roasted red peppers for enhanced smoky flavor
- Blend soup until silky smooth for a luxurious texture
- Garnish with crème fraîche instead of cream for a tangier finish

Nutritional Values: Calories: 200, Fat: 15g, Carbs: 15g, Protein: 3g, Sugar: 8g

GINGER MISO SWEET POTATO BISQUE

Preparation Time: 20 min
Cooking Time: 40 min
Mode of Cooking: Stovetop
Servings: 5
Ingredients:

- 2 lbs. sweet potatoes, peeled and cubed
- 2 Tbsp miso paste
- 4 cups water
- 1 Tbsp grated fresh ginger
- 1 onion, diced

- 2 Tbsp olive oil
- 1 tsp sesame oil
- 1/4 tsp ground cinnamon
- 1/4 tsp cayenne pepper
- 1/2 cup light coconut milk
- Green onions, sliced for garnish

Directions:

1. Heat olive and sesame oils in a pot over medium heat
2. Sauté onions until translucent
3. Add grated ginger, cinnamon, and cayenne pepper, stirring for a few seconds
4. Add sweet potatoes and water, bring to boil
5. Reduce heat and simmer until sweet potatoes are tender, about 30 min
6. Stir in miso paste and coconut milk until well combined
7. Puree the soup until smooth
8. Serve hot, garnished with green onions

Tips:

- Dissolve miso paste in a small amount of warm water before adding to avoid clumps
- Top with toasted sesame seeds for a nutty flavor
- Add a swirl of chili oil for a spicy kick

Nutritional Values: Calories: 255, Fat: 9g, Carbs: 39g, Protein: 5g, Sugar: 7g

HERBED WHITE BEAN AND KALE SOUP

Preparation Time: 10 min
Cooking Time: 3 hr
Mode of Cooking: Slow Cooker
Servings: 8
Ingredients:

- 1 lb. dried white beans, soaked overnight and drained
- 2 quarts vegetable broth
- 1 bay leaf
- 1 tsp dried oregano
- 1 tsp dried thyme

- 1 large carrot, chopped
- 2 stalks celery, chopped
- 1 onion, chopped
- 3 cloves garlic, minced
- 4 cups chopped kale
- Salt and pepper to taste
- Grated Parmesan cheese for garnish

Directions:

1. Place all ingredients except kale and Parmesan in the slow cooker
2. Cook on low for about 3 hr or until beans are tender
3. In the last 30 min of cooking, add chopped kale
4. Discard bay leaf
5. Season with salt and pepper
6. Serve hot, garnished with grated Parmesan cheese

Tips:

- Prepare this soup a day ahead for flavors to meld beautifully
- Use high-quality Parmesan for best flavor
- Add a splash of lemon juice before serving to enhance the flavors

Nutritional Values: Calories: 215, Fat: 1.5g, Carbs: 38g, Protein: 14g, Sugar: 3g

SPICY LENTIL AND SPINACH STEW

Preparation Time: 15 min
Cooking Time: 25 min
Mode of Cooking: Stovetop
Servings: 4
Ingredients:

- 1 Tbsp olive oil
- 1 large onion, diced
- 2 cloves garlic, minced
- 1 tsp ground cumin
- 1/2 tsp ground coriander
- 1/4 tsp ground turmeric
- 1/4 tsp cayenne pepper

- 1 cup red lentils
- 4 cups vegetable broth
- 2 cups fresh spinach, chopped
- Salt and pepper to taste
- Greek yogurt for serving

Directions:

1. Heat olive oil in a large pot over medium heat
2. Add onion and cook until soft
3. Add garlic and spices, cooking for another minute
4. Stir in red lentils and vegetable broth, bring to a boil
5. Reduce heat to medium-low and simmer until lentils are tender, about 20 min
6. Stir in chopped spinach until wilted
7. Season with salt and pepper
8. Serve hot with a dollop of Greek yogurt on top

Tips:

- Rinse lentils thoroughly before cooking to remove any impurities
- Serve with warm naan or pita bread for a hearty meal
- Add lemon zest for a fresh flavor boost

Nutritional Values: Calories: 375, Fat: 5g, Carbs: 62g, Protein: 25g, Sugar: 3g

ROASTED BEET AND GINGER SOUP

Preparation Time: 20 min.
Cooking Time: 1 hr.
Mode of Cooking: Oven and Stovetop
Servings: 6
Ingredients:

- 3 medium beets, peeled and quartered
- 1 Tbsp coconut oil
- 2 Tbsp grated fresh ginger
- 1 large onion, chopped
- 2 cloves garlic, minced
- 4 cups vegetable broth
- Salt and pepper to taste

- 1 Tbsp apple cider vinegar
- 2 Tbsp Greek yogurt for garnish

Directions:

1. Preheat oven to 400°F (204°C)
2. Toss beets in coconut oil and roast for 40 min. or until tender
3. Heat a pot on medium, add ginger, onion, and garlic, cook until onion is soft
4. Add roasted beets and vegetable broth, bring to boil then simmer for 20 min.
5. Puree the mixture until smooth
6. Stir in apple cider vinegar, season with salt and pepper

Tips:

- Garnish with a dollop of Greek yogurt and dill
- You can roast extra beets for other uses during the week
- Add more ginger if you prefer a spicier soup

Nutritional Values: Calories: 98, Fat: 3g, Carbs: 16g, Protein: 2g, Sugar: 11g

COMFORTING BROTHS

GOLDEN TURMERIC CHICKEN BROTH

Preparation Time: 15 min
Cooking Time: 1 hr 30 min
Mode of Cooking: Simmering
Servings: 4
Ingredients:

- 1 lb. organic chicken bones
- 2 qt. water
- 1 large onion, quartered
- 3 garlic cloves, smashed
- 1 inch ginger, sliced
- 2 tsp turmeric powder
- 1 carrot, chopped
- 2 celery stalks, chopped
- 10 black peppercorns

- 1 bay leaf
- 1 tsp salt

Directions:

1. Combine chicken bones, water, onion, garlic, ginger, turmeric, carrot, celery, peppercorns, and bay leaf in a large pot and bring to a boil
2. Reduce heat and simmer gently for 1 hr 30 min, skimming foam as necessary
3. Strain the broth, season with salt, and serve warm or store after cooling.

Tips:

- Add a pinch of freshly ground black pepper to enhance turmeric absorption and spice up the flavor
- Store broth in the refrigerator for up to 5 days or freeze in portions for up to 3 months

Nutritional Values: Calories: 40, Fat: 0.5g, Carbs: 3g, Protein: 6g, Sugar: 1g

HEALING GINGER MISO BROTH

Preparation Time: 10 min
Cooking Time: 25 min
Mode of Cooking: Simmering
Servings: 6
Ingredients:

- 4 cups vegetable broth
- 2 Tbsp miso paste
- 1 Tbsp freshly grated ginger
- 3 Tbsp tamari or soy sauce
- 1 tsp sesame oil
- 2 green onions, sliced
- 1 Tbsp nori seaweed, torn into pieces
- 1 tsp sesame seeds

Directions:

1. Warm the vegetable broth in a pot over medium heat
2. Dissolve the miso paste in a small amount of warm broth, then return it to the pot
3. Add ginger, tamari, sesame oil, and simmer for 20 min

4. Serve topped with green onions, nori, and sesame seeds.

Tips:

- Experiment with different types of miso (such as white or red) for varying flavors and health benefits
- Garnish with fresh cilantro for an extra herbal note

Nutritional Values: Calories: 55, Fat: 2g, Carbs: 6g, Protein: 3g, Sugar: 2g

SOOTHING LEMON THYME CHICKEN BROTH

Preparation Time: 20 min
Cooking Time: 3 hr
Mode of Cooking: Simmering
Servings: 6
Ingredients:

- 1 whole chicken carcass, leftover from roasted chicken
- 3 qt. water
- 1 onion, chopped
- 2 carrots, sliced
- 2 lemons, halved
- 4 sprigs thyme
- 2 cloves garlic, minced
- Salt to taste
- Freshly ground black pepper

Directions:

1. Place chicken carcass, water, onion, carrots, lemons, thyme, and garlic in a large pot and bring to a gentle boil
2. Reduce to a simmer and cook uncovered for 3 hr, adding more water if necessary
3. Season with salt and black pepper, strain and serve or store.

Tips:

- Use organic lemons for a pesticide-free broth and enhanced flavor

- Squeeze the cooked lemons into the broth before straining for an extra burst of lemony sharpness
- Add a pinch of cayenne pepper for a warming kick

Nutritional Values: Calories: 70, Fat: 1.5g, Carbs: 5g, Protein: 10g, Sugar: 1g

RICH BEEF BONE BROTH

Preparation Time: 10 min
Cooking Time: 48 hr
Mode of Cooking: Slow Cooking
Servings: 8
Ingredients:

- 2 lb. beef bones, roasted
- 4 qt. water
- 1 Tbsp apple cider vinegar
- 3 carrots, chopped
- 3 stalks celery, chopped
- 2 onions, quartered
- 5 cloves garlic
- 1 bunch parsley
- 10 black peppercorns
- 2 bay leaves
- Salt to taste

Directions:

1. Place roasted beef bones into a slow cooker and cover with water
2. Add apple cider vinegar, carrots, celery, onions, garlic, parsley, peppercorns, and bay leaves
3. Cook on low for 48 hr
4. Strain the broth, season with salt, and serve or store.

Tips:

- Roasting the bones prior to simmering enhances the flavor and color of the broth
- Add vinegar to help extract nutrients from the bones

- Freeze in ice cube trays for easy use in future recipes

Nutritional Values: Calories: 50, Fat: 2g, Carbs: 2g, Protein: 6g, Sugar: 1g

EXOTIC SAFFRON VEGETABLE BROTH

Preparation Time: 15 min
Cooking Time: 40 min
Mode of Cooking: Boiling
Servings: 4
Ingredients:

- 4 cups vegetable stock
- 1 pinch saffron threads
- 1 fennel bulb, chopped
- 1 leek, white part only, sliced
- ½ cup sliced shiitake mushrooms
- 1 tsp coriander seeds
- 1 star anise
- Salt to taste
- Fresh ground black pepper

Directions:

1. Bring vegetable stock to a boil and add saffron, fennel, leek, mushrooms, coriander seeds, and star anise
2. Reduce heat and simmer for 40 min
3. Season with salt and pepper, strain and serve warm.

Tips:

- Saffron not only adds a luxurious aroma and golden hue but is also known for its anti-inflammatory properties
- Pair this broth with a splash of white wine for a deeper flavor
- Strain and use as a base for risottos or soups for added depth and flavor

Nutritional Values: Calories: 30, Fat: 0g, Carbs: 6g, Protein: 2g, Sugar: 2g

SOOTHING GINGER MISO BROTH

Preparation Time: 10 min
Cooking Time: 30 min
Mode of Cooking: Boiling
Servings: 6
Ingredients:

- 6 cups water
- 4 Tbsp miso paste
- 2-inch piece of ginger, sliced
- 2 cloves garlic, thinly sliced
- 1 Tbsp tamari sauce
- 3 green onions, chopped
- 1 Tbsp sesame oil
- 1 tsp chili flakes (optional)
- Seaweed, optional for garnish

Directions:

1. Heat water in a pot over medium-high heat until just simmering
2. Add ginger, garlic, and simmer for 20 min
3. Reduce heat to low, add miso paste, tamari, sesame oil, and chili flakes, stirring until miso is dissolved
4. Serve hot, garnished with green onions and optional seaweed

Tips:

- Do not boil after adding miso to preserve its probiotic benefits
- Add tofu cubes for a protein boost

Nutritional Values: Calories: 35, Fat: 2g, Carbs: 3g, Protein: 2g, Sugar: 1g

CREAMY SOUPS

SILKEN BUTTERNUT SQUASH SOUP

Preparation Time: 20 min
Cooking Time: 50 min
Mode of Cooking: Simmering
Servings: 4
Ingredients:

- 1 medium butternut squash, peeled and cubed
- 1 large onion, finely chopped
- 2 cloves garlic, minced
- 3 cups vegetable broth
- 1 cup coconut milk
- 1 tsp ground nutmeg
- Salt and fresh ground pepper to taste
- 2 Tbsp olive oil

Directions:

1. Heat olive oil in a large pot over medium heat
2. Add onion and garlic, sauté until soft
3. Add cubed butternut squash and cook for 10 min
4. Pour in vegetable broth and bring to a boil
5. Reduce heat and simmer until squash is tender, about 40 min
6. Remove from heat and blend with an immersion blender until smooth
7. Stir in coconut milk and nutmeg
8. Season with salt and pepper and heat through

Tips:

- Serve hot topped with a dollop of coconut cream for added richness
- Stir in a pinch of cayenne pepper for a spicy kick
- Decorate with fresh parsley for color contrast

Nutritional Values: Calories: 180, Fat: 7g, Carbs: 27g, Protein: 3g, Sugar: 8g

CREAMY MUSHROOM AND LEEK SOUP

Preparation Time: 15 min
Cooking Time: 30 min
Mode of Cooking: Simmering
Servings: 6
Ingredients:

- 2 Tbsp unsalted butter
- 1 lb sliced mixed mushrooms (shiitake, portobello, button)

- 2 leeks, white and light green parts only, thinly sliced
- 4 cups chicken or vegetable broth
- 1 cup heavy cream
- 2 tsp fresh thyme leaves
- Salt and black pepper to taste

Directions:

1. Melt butter in a large saucepan over medium heat
2. Add leeks and sauté until softened
3. Increase heat, add mushrooms and cook until golden
4. Pour in broth and bring to a boil
5. Reduce heat, add thyme, and simmer for 20 min
6. Blend soup partly, leaving some mushroom pieces whole for texture
7. Add cream, and simmer for another 10 min
8. Season with salt and pepper

Tips:

- Garnish with extra thyme sprigs and serve with a crusty bread
- For a lighter version, replace heavy cream with full-fat coconut milk

Nutritional Values: Calories: 210, Fat: 18g, Carbs: 12g, Protein: 6g, Sugar: 4g

GOLDEN CAULIFLOWER VELVET SOUP

Preparation Time: 10 min
Cooking Time: 25 min
Mode of Cooking: Simmering
Servings: 5
Ingredients:

- 1 head cauliflower, broken into florets
- 3 Tbsp extra virgin olive oil
- 1 onion, chopped
- 2 cloves garlic, minced
- 1 tsp turmeric powder
- 5 cups vegetable stock
- 1 cup cashew nuts, soaked and drained

- Salt and pepper to taste

Directions:

1. Heat olive in a large pot over medium heat
2. Add onion and garlic and sauté until translucent
3. Stir in turmeric and cook for 1 min
4. Add cauliflower, cashew nuts, and vegetable stock
5. Bring to a simmer and cook until cauliflower is soft, about 20 min
6. Blend until smooth and creamy
7. Season with salt and pepper

Tips:

- Garnish with a sprinkle of chopped coriander and toasted cashew nuts for texture and flavor
- Stir in a spoonful of nutritional yeast for a cheesy flavor without the dairy

Nutritional Values: Calories: 154, Fat: 9g, Carbs: 15g, Protein: 6g, Sugar: 5g

CARROT AND GINGER CREAM SOUP

Preparation Time: 10 min
Cooking Time: 35 min
Mode of Cooking: Simmering
Servings: 4
Ingredients:

- 2 Tbsp coconut oil
- 1 lb carrots, peeled and diced
- 2 tsp grated ginger
- 1 onion, diced
- 4 cups vegetable broth
- 1 cup coconut milk
- Salt and freshly ground black pepper to taste
- 1 Tbsp lemon juice

Directions:

1. Heat coconut oil in a large pot over medium heat
2. Add onion and sauté until clear

3. Add ginger and carrots and cook for 5 min, stirring occasionally
4. Pour in broth and bring to a boil
5. Reduce to a simmer, cover, and cook until carrots are tender, about 25 min
6. Blend the soup until smooth
7. Return to the pot, add coconut milk and lemon juice, and heat through
8. Season with salt and pepper

Tips:

- Offer a swirl of coconut cream and a sprinkle of chopped scallions for extra flavor and a visual appeal
- Add a pinch of cayenne pepper for a spicy version

Nutritional Values: Calories: 162, Fat: 11g, Carbs: 16g, Protein: 2g, Sugar: 6g

Avocado and Cucumber Chilled Soup

Preparation Time: 15 min
Cooking Time: none
Mode of Cooking: Chilling
Servings: 4
Ingredients:

- 2 ripe avocados, peeled and pitted
- 1 cucumber, peeled and chopped
- 1 small onion, chopped
- 1 clove garlic, minced
- 2 cups plain yogurt
- 2 Tbsp lime juice
- 1/2 cup fresh cilantro, chopped
- Salt and pepper to taste
- 1 cup cold water

Directions:

1. Combine avocados, cucumber, onion, and garlic in a blender
2. Add yogurt, lime juice, cilantro, and cold water
3. Blend until smooth
4. Season with salt and pepper

5. Chill in the refrigerator for at least 2 hr before serving

Tips:

- Offer a sprinkle of chili flakes for heat and diced tomatoes for freshness just before serving
- Blend in a tablespoon of olive oil for a smoother texture

Nutritional Values: Calories: 190, Fat: 15g, Carbs: 12g, Protein: 4g, Sugar: 7g

Velvety Beet and Coconut Soup

Preparation Time: 15 min.
Cooking Time: 35 min.
Mode of Cooking: Stovetop
Servings: 4
Ingredients:

- 2 medium beets, peeled and diced
- 1 Tbsp coconut oil
- 1 onion, chopped
- 2 cloves garlic, minced
- 1 tsp ground ginger
- 1 can (14 oz.) coconut milk
- 2 cups vegetable broth
- Salt and pepper to taste
- Fresh cilantro for garnish

Directions:

1. Melt coconut oil in a large pot over medium heat
2. Add onion and garlic, sauté until translucent
3. Stir in ginger and diced beets, cook for 5 min.
4. Pour in coconut milk and vegetable broth, bring to a boil
5. Reduce heat to simmer, cover, and cook until beets are tender, about 30 min.
6. Blend the soup in batches in a blender until smooth
7. Return soup to the pot, reheat gently, season with salt and pepper
8. Serve garnished with fresh cilantro

Tips:

- Add a squeeze of lime for a tangy twist
- Serve with a dollop of yogurt for extra creaminess
- Top with toasted coconut flakes for added texture

Nutritional Values: Calories: 250, Fat: 18g, Carbs: 21g, Protein: 3g, Sugar: 11g

CHAPTER 7: MAIN DISHES

Imagine this: It's a tranquil evening, and the gentle aroma of spices fills your kitchen. There's something incredibly soothing about preparing a meal that not only tantalizes your taste buds but also nourishes your body deeply. Welcome to the heart of our culinary journey—main dishes that are as healing as they are delicious. This chapter isn't just a collection of recipes; it's your gateway to transforming everyday meals into powerful tools for reducing inflammation, enhancing your energy, and enriching your life with joyous health.

Navigating an anti-inflammatory diet often converges beautifully in the realm of main dishes. Here, vibrant vegetables, lean proteins, wholesome grains, and heart-healthy fats dance together in a symphony of flavors and textures designed to delight while defying inflammation. Whether it's a succulently roasted chicken seasoned with turmeric and thyme, a hearty vegetarian chili brimming with legumes and spices, or a delicate fillet of salmon adorned with a ginger glaze, the recipes you will discover here promise satisfaction on every level.

Every dish tells a story. A story of transformation, where simple ingredients come together to create something extraordinary—not just in taste but in its capability to promote health and well-being. As you explore these recipes, remember that each ingredient plays a pivotal role in reducing inflammatory responses in your body, helping you to not only feel better but to thrive.

Think of the warmth a well-cooked meal brings to your dining table, the smiles it gathers, and the wellness it fosters. As you delve into the flavors curated within these pages, you're not just feeding your stomach; you're nurturing your soul.

So, let's don our aprons with enthusiasm and stir up some magic in our pots and pans. Every recipe here is designed to be straightforward, ensuring that you spend less time in the kitchen and more time enjoying the fruits of your labor with friends and family. After all, good food is not merely about taste—it's an essential component of a vibrant, energetic life. Here's to making every meal a testament to your health and happiness.

POULTRY DISHES

TUSCAN GARLIC TURMERIC CHICKEN

Preparation Time: 15 min
Cooking Time: 30 min
Mode of Cooking: Baking
Servings: 4

Ingredients:

- 4 chicken breasts, boneless and skinless
- 1 Tbsp extra virgin olive oil
- 2 cloves garlic, minced
- 1 tsp turmeric powder
- 1 tsp Italian seasoning
- ½ cup sun-dried tomatoes, chopped
- 1 cup spinach, fresh
- 1 cup low-sodium chicken broth
- ½ cup coconut milk
- Salt and pepper to taste

Directions:

1. Season chicken breasts with salt, pepper, turmeric, and Italian seasoning

2. In a skillet, heat olive oil over medium heat and add garlic until fragrant

3. Add chicken and sear on each side for 3-4 min

4. Transfer chicken to a baking dish, add sun-dried tomatoes and spinach around chicken

5. Mix chicken broth and coconut milk and pour over the chicken

6. Bake in preheated oven at 375°F (190°C) for 25 min

Tips:

- Include a sprinkle of chopped fresh basil for a fresh touch

- Serve with a side of quinoa or roasted vegetables

Nutritional Values: Calories: 310, Fat: 13g, Carbs: 8g, Protein: 38g, Sugar: 4g

SPICY MAPLE DIJON GLAZED CHICKEN

Preparation Time: 10 min
Cooking Time: 20 min
Mode of Cooking: Pan-frying
Servings: 4
Ingredients:

- 4 chicken thighs, bone-in and skin-on
- 2 Tbsp Dijon mustard
- 2 Tbsp pure maple syrup
- 1 Tbsp apple cider vinegar
- 1 tsp smoked paprika
- ½ tsp red pepper flakes
- Salt and black pepper to taste
- 1 Tbsp olive oil

Directions:

1. Mix Dijon mustard, maple syrup, apple cider vinegar, smoked paprika, red pepper flakes, salt, and black pepper in a bowl

2. Heat olive oil in a skillet over medium-high heat

3. Add chicken thighs skin-side down and cook until crispy, about 7 min

4. Flip chicken, reduce heat to medium, and brush the maple Dijon mixture over the chicken

5. Cover and cook for another 10-12 min

Tips:

- Brush with additional glaze before serving for extra flavor

- Pair with steamed green beans or a kale salad for a balanced meal

Nutritional Values: Calories: 475, Fat: 29g, Carbs: 15g, Protein: 35g, Sugar: 12g

LEMON HERB ROASTED CHICKEN

Preparation Time: 20 min
Cooking Time: 1 hr
Mode of Cooking: Roasting
Servings: 6
Ingredients:

- 1 whole chicken (approximately 4 lb)
- 2 lemons, one juiced and one sliced
- 4 garlic cloves, crushed
- 2 Tbsp fresh rosemary, chopped
- 2 Tbsp fresh thyme, chopped
- 3 Tbsp olive oil
- Salt and black pepper to taste
- 1 lb small potatoes, halved

Directions:

1. Preheat oven to 425°F (220°C)

2. In a bowl, combine lemon juice, crushed garlic, rosemary, thyme, olive oil, salt, and pepper

3. Place chicken in a roasting pan, rub the herb mixture all over it, and stuff the cavity with sliced lemons

4. Scatter potatoes around the chicken in the pan

5. Roast in the oven for about 1 hr or until the chicken is golden and cooked through

Tips:

- Let the chicken rest for 10 min before carving
- Serve with the roasted potatoes and a side of steamed vegetables for a complete meal

Nutritional Values: Calories: 510, Fat: 24g, Carbs: 22g, Protein: 50g, Sugar: 1g

SZECHUAN PEPPERCORN CHICKEN STIR-FRY

Preparation Time: 15 min
Cooking Time: 10 min
Mode of Cooking: Stir-frying
Servings: 4
Ingredients:

- 2 lb chicken breast, cut into strips
- 2 Tbsp Szechuan peppercorns, crushed
- 1 red bell pepper, julienned
- 1 green bell pepper, julienned
- 1 Tbsp ginger, minced
- 2 Tbsp soy sauce
- 1 Tbsp sesame oil
- 2 Tbsp hoisin sauce
- 1 Tbsp honey
- 1 tsp cornstarch dissolved in 2 Tbsp water
- 2 Tbsp vegetable oil

Directions:

1. Heat vegetable oil in a wok or large skillet over high heat
2. Add chicken strips and stir-fry until nearly cooked, about 5 min
3. Add ginger and bell peppers, cook for an additional 3 min
4. Mix soy sauce, sesame oil, hoisin sauce, honey, and cornstarch mixture in a small bowl and add to the wok
5. Stir well and cook until sauce is thickened and chicken is cooked through

Tips:

- Serve over steamed rice or noodles

- Garnish with sesame seeds and fresh cilantro for enhanced flavor

Nutritional Values: Calories: 370, Fat: 12g, Carbs: 18g, Protein: 44g, Sugar: 10g

MOROCCAN CHICKEN TAGINE

Preparation Time: 30 min
Cooking Time: 1 hr
Mode of Cooking: Simmering
Servings: 6
Ingredients:

- 3 lb chicken thighs, bone-in and skin-on
- 2 Tbsp olive oil
- 1 large onion, chopped
- 3 garlic cloves, minced
- 2 tsp ground cumin
- 2 tsp ground coriander
- 1 tsp ground cinnamon
- 1 tsp turmeric
- ½ tsp cayenne pepper
- 1 cup dried apricots, chopped
- 1 can (14 oz) diced tomatoes
- 1 can (15 oz) chickpeas, drained and rinsed
- 2 cups chicken broth
- Salt and black pepper to taste
- Fresh cilantro for garnish

Directions:

1. Heat olive oil in a large pot or tagine over medium heat
2. Add onions and garlic, sauté until soft
3. Add chicken thighs and brown on both sides
4. Stir in cumin, coriander, cinnamon, turmeric, and cayenne pepper
5. Add apricots, tomatoes, chickpeas, and chicken broth
6. Bring to a boil, then reduce heat to low, cover, and simmer for about 1 hr

Tips:

- Garnish with fresh cilantro before serving

- Serve with couscous or flatbread to soak up the delicious sauce

Nutritional Values: Calories: 450, Fat: 22g, Carbs: 30g, Protein: 35g, Sugar: 15g

TURMERIC GINGER CHICKEN STIR-FRY

Preparation Time: 15 min.
Cooking Time: 20 min.
Mode of Cooking: Sauté
Servings: 4
Ingredients:

- 2 lb. boneless, skinless chicken breast, thinly sliced
- 1 red bell pepper, julienned
- 1 green bell pepper, julienned
- 1 yellow onion, sliced
- 2 cloves garlic, minced
- 2 Tbsp fresh ginger, minced
- 1 tsp turmeric powder
- 1 Tbsp olive oil
- 1 Tbsp sesame oil
- 2 Tbsp soy sauce
- 1 Tbsp honey
- 1 tsp black pepper
- ¼ cup fresh cilantro, chopped
- 2 tsp sesame seeds

Directions:

1. Heat olive oil and sesame oil in a large skillet over medium-high heat
2. Add garlic and ginger, sauté for 2 min.
3. Incorporate chicken and turmeric, cook until chicken is nearly done, about 15 min.
4. Add bell peppers and onion, cook for another 5 min.
5. Stir in soy sauce, honey, and black pepper, cook for 2-3 min.
6. Garnish with cilantro and sesame seeds

Tips:

- Serve over brown rice or quinoa for a complete meal

- Can be made gluten-free by using tamari instead of soy sauce
- Add chili flakes for extra spice

Nutritional Values: Calories: 295, Fat: 12g, Carbs: 15g, Protein: 34g, Sugar: 8g

MEAT DISHES

SPICED LAMB TAGINE WITH APRICOTS AND ALMONDS

Preparation Time: 20 min
Cooking Time: 2 hr
Mode of Cooking: Slow Cooking
Servings: 6
Ingredients:

- 2 lb. lamb shoulder, cut into 2-inch pieces
- 1 large onion, finely chopped
- 3 garlic cloves, minced
- 1 Tbsp ginger, freshly grated
- 2 tsp cumin, ground
- 2 tsp coriander, ground
- 1 tsp cinnamon, ground
- 1/2 tsp turmeric, ground
- 1/4 tsp cayenne pepper
- 1 can (14 oz.) diced tomatoes
- 1 quart beef stock
- 1 cup dried apricots, sliced
- 1/2 cup almonds, toasted
- 2 Tbsp honey
- Salt and pepper to taste
- Fresh cilantro tor garnish

Directions:

1. Trim excess fat from lamb pieces and pat dry
2. Heat a spoon of oil in a large tagine or heavy-based pot over medium heat and brown lamb pieces on all sides, then remove and set aside
3. In the same pot, add onions, garlic, and ginger, cooking until softened

4. Return lamb to the pot along with all spices and cook for 1 to 2 min, stirring constantly

5. Add tomatoes and stock, bring to a simmer, then reduce heat to low, cover, and allow to cook for 1.5 hr

6. Add apricots and honey, continue to simmer for another 30 min.

7. Toast almonds in a dry skillet until golden, set aside

Tips:

- To bring out more flavors, ensure lamb is well seared before slow cooking
- Serve with couscous or flatbread for a complete meal
- Garnish with fresh cilantro and toasted almonds before serving

Nutritional Values: Calories: 420, Fat: 24g, Carbs: 28g, Protein: 27g, Sugar: 20g

HERB CRUSTED PRIME RIB WITH HORSERADISH CREAM

Preparation Time: 15 min
Cooking Time: 3 hr 30 min
Mode of Cooking: Roasting
Servings: 8
Ingredients:

- 5 lb. prime rib roast
- 1 Tbsp kosher salt
- 2 tsp black pepper, crushed
- 4 garlic cloves, minced
- 2 Tbsp rosemary, finely chopped
- 2 Tbsp thyme, finely chopped
- 3 Tbsp olive oil
- For Horseradish Cream: 1 cup sour cream
- 1/4 cup horseradish
- 1 Tbsp Dijon mustard
- 1 tsp apple cider vinegar
- Salt and pepper to taste

Directions:

1. Preheat oven to 350°F (175°C)

2. Mix garlic, rosemary, thyme, salt, pepper, and olive oil to create a paste

3. Rub the paste evenly over the surface of the prime rib

4. Place prime rib in a roasting pan, fat side up, and roast for about 3 hr 30 min, or until the meat reaches an internal temperature of 130°F (54°C) for medium-rare

5. Combine ingredients for horseradish cream in a bowl and chill until serving

Tips:

- Allow the roast to rest for at least 20 min before slicing to retain juices
- Serve with a dollop of horseradish cream for added zest

Nutritional Values: Calories: 690, Fat: 54g, Carbs: 3g, Protein: 46g, Sugar: 1g

BEEF ROULADEN WITH PICKLE AND MUSTARD FILLING

Preparation Time: 30 min
Cooking Time: 1 hr 30 min
Mode of Cooking: Braising
Servings: 4
Ingredients:

- 4 slices beef top round, thin-cut
- 4 tsp Dijon mustard
- 4 dill pickles, sliced longitudinally
- 1 onion, thinly sliced
- 4 slices bacon
- 1 cup beef broth
- 1/2 cup red wine
- Salt and pepper to taste
- Fresh parsley, chopped for garnish

Directions:

1. Spread each slice of beef with mustard and season with salt and pepper

2. Place a slice of bacon, a few pickle slices, and some onion at one end of each beef slice and roll up tightly, securing with toothpicks

3. Brown roulades in a skillet with a little oil, then remove

4. Deglaze skillet with red wine and add beef broth

5. Return roulades to the skillet, cover, and simmer gently for about 1 hr 30 min

6. Remove toothpicks and sprinkle with fresh parsley before serving

Tips:

- Thin cuts of beef work best for roulades for easier rolling and cooking

- Use cornichons for a sharper taste in place of standard pickles

- Serve with potato dumplings or spaetzle to soak up the rich sauce

Nutritional Values: Calories: 320, Fat: 16g, Carbs: 7g, Protein: 35g, Sugar: 2g

PORK TENDERLOIN WITH PLUM SAUCE

Preparation Time: 15 min
Cooking Time: 45 min
Mode of Cooking: Roasting
Servings: 6
Ingredients:

- 2 lb. pork tenderloin
- Salt and pepper to taste
- For Plum Sauce: 8 ripe plums, pitted and chopped
- 1 red onion, finely chopped
- 1/2 cup red wine
- 2 Tbsp balsamic vinegar
- 1 Tbsp honey
- 1 tsp ginger, minced
- 1 clove garlic, minced
- 1 cinnamon stick
- Salt to taste

Directions:

1. Preheat the oven to 375°F (190°C)

2. Season the pork tenderloins with salt and pepper

3. Roast in the oven until the pork reaches an internal temperature of 145°F (63°C), about 45 min

4. While pork is roasting, combine plums, onion, red wine, balsamic vinegar, honey, ginger, garlic, and cinnamon stick in a saucepan over medium heat

5. Simmer until the sauce thickens and plums are broken down, about 30 min, remove the cinnamon stick before serving

Tips:

- Pair with roasted vegetables for a balanced meal

- Plum sauce can be made in advance and stored in the fridge

- Slice tenderloin thinly to serve and drizzle with warm plum sauce

Nutritional Values: Calories: 295, Fat: 8g, Carbs: 26g, Protein: 30g, Sugar: 19g

BALSAMIC GLAZED STEAK ROLLS

Preparation Time: 25 min
Cooking Time: 15 min
Mode of Cooking: Grilling
Servings: 4
Ingredients:

- 1 lb. flank steak, thinly sliced
- 2 bell peppers, thinly sliced
- 1 zucchini, thinly sliced
- 1 carrot, thinly sliced
- 2 Tbsp olive oil
- 3 Tbsp balsamic vinegar
- 2 Tbsp soy sauce
- 1 Tbsp honey
- 1 clove garlic, minced
- Salt and pepper to taste

Directions:

1. Pound flank steak slices to 1/4 inch thickness and season with salt and pepper

2. Mix balsamic vinegar, soy sauce, honey, garlic, and oil to create a marinade

3. Brush this marinade over the steak slices

4. Lay out the steak slices and top each with slices of bell pepper, zucchini, and carrot

5. Roll up tightly and secure with toothpicks

6. Grill on medium-high heat, turning occasionally, until browned and cooked through, about 15 min

Tips:

- Vegetables inside the steak rolls should be sliced very thin to cook evenly with the steak

- Leftover marinade can be boiled for a couple of minutes and used as a sauce

- Serve steak rolls with a side of mashed potatoes or rice for a complete meal

Nutritional Values: Calories: 310, Fat: 15g, Carbs: 12g, Protein: 28g, Sugar: 8g

TURMERIC-SPICED LAMB CHOPS WITH CILANTRO GREMOLATA

Preparation Time: 15 min
Cooking Time: 20 min
Mode of Cooking: Grilling
Servings: 4
Ingredients:

- 4 lamb chops, 1-inch thick
- 1 Tbsp olive oil
- 1 Tsp ground turmeric
- 1 Tsp ground cumin
- 1 Tsp smoked paprika
- Salt and black pepper to taste
- For Gremolata: ½ cup chopped cilantro
- Zest of 1 lemon
- 2 cloves garlic, minced
- 1 Tbsp lemon juice
- 2 Tbsp extra virgin olive oil

Directions:

1. Rub lamb chops with olive oil, turmeric, cumin, paprika, salt, and black pepper

2. Preheat grill to medium-high (about 450°F or 232°C)

3. Grill lamb chops for 10 min on one side, then flip and continue grilling for another 10 min

4. In a small bowl, mix together cilantro, lemon zest, garlic, lemon juice, and olive oil to create the gremolata

5. Serve lamb chops topped with gremolata

Tips:

- Serve with a side of grilled vegetables for a wholesome meal

- Always let meat rest for 5 min before serving to retain its juices

Nutritional Values: Calories: 398, Fat: 27g, Carbs: 2g, Protein: 34g, Sugar: 0g

FISH AND SEAFOOD

GINGER-LIME BAKED COD

Preparation Time: 15 min.
Cooking Time: 20 min.
Mode of Cooking: Baking
Servings: 4
Ingredients:

- 4 cod fillets, about 6 oz. each
- 2 Tbsp olive oil
- Zest and juice of 1 lime
- 1 Tbsp fresh ginger, minced
- 2 cloves garlic, minced
- 2 Tbsp fresh cilantro, chopped
- Salt and pepper to taste
- Lime wedges for serving

Directions:

1. Preheat oven to 400°F (200°C)

2. In a bowl, mix olive oil, lime zest, lime juice, ginger, garlic, and cilantro

3. Season cod fillets with salt and pepper and place in a baking dish

4. Pour the lime-ginger mixture over the cod fillets

5. Bake in the preheated oven for 20 min., or until the fish flakes easily with a fork

Tips:

- Serve with extra lime wedges for added zest
- Pair with a side of steamed asparagus for a perfect meal

Nutritional Values: Calories: 190, Fat: 6g, Carbs: 2g, Protein: 30g, Sugar: 0g

CHILI GARLIC SHRIMP SKEWERS

Preparation Time: 10 min.
Cooking Time: 8 min.
Mode of Cooking: Grilling
Servings: 4
Ingredients:

- 24 large shrimp, peeled and deveined
- 1 Tbsp olive oil
- 2 tsp chili powder
- 3 cloves garlic, minced
- Salt to taste
- Fresh parsley, chopped for garnish

Directions:

1. Preheat grill to medium-high heat
2. In a bowl, toss the shrimp with olive oil, chili powder, and minced garlic
3. Thread shrimp onto skewers
4. Grill for 3-4 min. per side, or until shrimp is opaque and cooked through

Tips:

- Sprinkle with fresh parsley before serving for a fresh touch
- Serve over a bed of mixed greens for a light meal

Nutritional Values: Calories: 120, Fat: 3g, Carbs: 1g, Protein: 18g, Sugar: 0g

MEDITERRANEAN SALMON WITH FENNEL AND OLIVES

Preparation Time: 20 min.
Cooking Time: 25 min.
Mode of Cooking: Roasting
Servings: 4
Ingredients:

- 4 salmon fillets, about 6 oz. each
- 1 bulb fennel, thinly sliced
- 1 cup cherry tomatoes, halved
- ½ cup Kalamata olives, pitted
- 2 Tbsp capers
- 1 lemon, sliced
- 3 Tbsp olive oil
- Salt and pepper to taste

Directions:

1. Preheat oven to 375°F (190°C)
2. Arrange fennel slices in a roasting pan and drizzle with 1 Tbsp olive oil
3. Place salmon fillets on top of the fennel
4. Scatter tomatoes, olives, and capers around the salmon
5. Top with lemon slices and drizzle with the remaining olive oil
6. Season with salt and pepper
7. Roast in the preheated oven for about 25 min., or until salmon is cooked through

Tips:

- Pair with a glass of crisp white wine for a refined experience
- Consider adding a sprinkle of fresh dill for an extra layer of flavor

Nutritional Values: Calories: 340, Fat: 22g, Carbs: 8g, Protein: 27g, Sugar: 3g

HERBED HADDOCK EN PAPILLOTE

Preparation Time: 20 min.
Cooking Time: 15 min.
Mode of Cooking: Baking
Servings: 4
Ingredients:

- 4 haddock fillets, about 6 oz. each
- 2 Tbsp fresh parsley, finely chopped
- 2 Tbsp fresh chives, finely chopped
- 1 lemon, sliced
- 2 Tbsp olive oil
- Salt and pepper to taste
- Parchment paper for wrapping

Directions:

1. Preheat oven to 400°F (200°C)
2. Cut 4 pieces of parchment paper large enough to wrap each fillet individually
3. Place a haddock fillet on each piece of parchment
4. Top each fillet with herbs, two lemon slices, and a drizzle of olive oil
5. Season with salt and pepper
6. Fold the paper over the fish, twisting the edges to seal
7. Bake for 15 min., or until the fish is cooked through

Tips:

- The en papillote method keeps the fish moist and flavorful
- Serve immediately to enjoy its aromatic steam when opened

Nutritional Values: Calories: 200, Fat: 9g, Carbs: 1g, Protein: 27g, Sugar: 0g

SPICY ORANGE GLAZED TILAPIA

Preparation Time: 10 min.
Cooking Time: 12 min.
Mode of Cooking: Pan Frying
Servings: 4
Ingredients:

- 4 tilapia fillets, about 6 oz. each
- Juice and zest of 2 oranges
- 1 Tbsp honey
- 1 tsp red chili flakes
- 1 Tbsp soy sauce
- 1 Tbsp olive oil
- Salt and pepper to taste

Directions:

1. Mix orange juice, orange zest, honey, red chili flakes, and soy sauce in a bowl
2. Heat olive oil in a skillet over medium heat
3. Season tilapia fillets with salt and pepper
4. Fry tilapia for about 3 min. per side, or until golden and nearly cooked through
5. Pour the orange glaze over the tilapia and cook for an additional 2 min. until the glaze thickens and the fish is fully cooked

Tips:

- The spicy-sweet glaze complements the mild flavor of tilapia beautifully
- Garnish with green onions for an extra pop of color and flavor

Nutritional Values: Calories: 220, Fat: 7g, Carbs: 10g, Protein: 29g, Sugar: 7g

CHILEAN SEA BASS WITH MANGO SALSA

Preparation Time: 25 min
Cooking Time: 20 min
Mode of Cooking: Baking
Servings: 4
Ingredients:

- 4 Chilean sea bass fillets, 6 oz each
- 1 Tbsp extra virgin olive oil
- Salt and pepper to taste
- 1 ripe mango, diced
- 1 small red onion, finely chopped
- 1 red bell pepper, diced
- 1 jalapeño, seeded and minced
- Juice of 1 lime

- 1/4 cup cilantro, chopped
- 1 tsp honey

Directions:

1. Preheat oven to 375°F (190°C)
2. Place the sea bass fillets on a baking sheet lined with parchment paper and brush with olive oil, season with salt and pepper
3. Bake in the preheated oven until the fish flakes easily with a fork, about 15-20 min
4. While the fish is baking, combine mango, red onion, red bell pepper, jalapeño, lime juice, cilantro, and honey in a bowl to make the salsa
5. Once fish is baked, top each fillet with a generous portion of mango salsa

Tips:

- Serve with a side of quinoa for a complete meal
- Garnish with extra cilantro for enhanced flavor

Nutritional Values: Calories: 290, Fat: 12g, Carbs: 18g, Protein: 23g, Sugar: 10g

HEARTY VEGETARIAN OPTIONS

MISO GLAZED EGGPLANT STEAKS

Preparation Time: 15 min
Cooking Time: 30 min
Mode of Cooking: Baking
Servings: 4
Ingredients:

- 2 large eggplants, sliced into 1-inch thick rounds
- 3 Tbsp white miso paste
- 2 Tbsp maple syrup
- 1 Tbsp rice vinegar
- 1 tsp sesame oil
- 2 cloves garlic, minced
- 1 Tbsp ginger, grated
- 1 Tbsp soy sauce

- 1 Tbsp olive oil
- 1 tsp chili flakes
- 1 Tbsp sesame seeds for garnish
- Fresh cilantro, chopped for garnish

Directions:

1. Preheat oven to 375°F (190°C)
2. Whisk together miso paste, maple syrup, rice vinegar, sesame oil, minced garlic, grated ginger, soy sauce, and chili flakes for the glaze
3. Brush both sides of each eggplant round with olive oil and arrange on a baking sheet
4. Generously apply miso glaze on each side
5. Bake for 30 min, flipping halfway through and reapplying the glaze
6. Garnish with sesame seeds and fresh cilantro

Tips:

- Serve with a side of brown rice or quinoa for a balanced meal
- Adding a sprinkle of toasted nori can enhance the umami flavor

Nutritional Values: Calories: 180, Fat: 7g, Carbs: 27g, Protein: 4g, Sugar: 13g

QUINOA AND BLACK BEAN STUFFED PEPPERS

Preparation Time: 20 min
Cooking Time: 35 min
Mode of Cooking: Baking
Servings: 6
Ingredients:

- 6 bell peppers, tops cut, and seeds removed
- 2 cups cooked quinoa
- 1 can black beans, drained and rinsed
- 1 cup corn kernels
- 1 medium onion, chopped
- 1 zucchini, diced
- 2 cloves garlic, minced
- 1 tsp cumin
- 1 tsp chili powder
- 1/2 tsp black pepper
- 1 cup shredded vegan cheese

- 2 Tbsp olive oil
- Fresh parsley, chopped for garnish

Directions:

1. Preheat oven to 350°F (177°C)
2. Heat olive oil in a skillet over medium heat
3. Sauté onion, garlic, and zucchini until softened
4. Stir in cumin, chili powder, and black pepper
5. Add cooked quinoa, black beans, and corn to the skillet, mixing well
6. Spoon the mixture into each bell pepper and top with vegan cheese
7. Place stuffed peppers in a baking dish and cook for 35 min
8. Garnish with fresh parsley

Tips:

- Experiment with different types of beans for variety in texture and flavor
- Adding a splash of lime juice can brighten the flavors

Nutritional Values: Calories: 310, Fat: 9g, Carbs: 49g, Protein: 14g, Sugar: 7g

CAULIFLOWER TIKKA MASALA

Preparation Time: 10 min
Cooking Time: 25 min
Mode of Cooking: Simmering
Servings: 4
Ingredients:

- 1 large cauliflower, cut into bite-sized florets
- 1 large onion, finely chopped
- 1 can diced tomatoes
- 1 can coconut milk
- 2 Tbsp tomato paste
- 2 Tbsp garam masala
- 1 Tbsp cumin
- 1 Tbsp coriander
- 1 tsp turmeric
- 1 Tbsp ginger, grated
- 3 cloves garlic, minced

- 2 Tbsp olive oil
- Fresh cilantro, chopped for garnish
- Salt to taste

Directions:

1. Heat olive oil in a large pan over medium heat
2. Sauté onion, garlic, and ginger until onion is translucent ♛ Add garam masala, cumin, coriander, and turmeric, cooking until fragrant
3. Stir in tomato paste, diced tomatoes, and cauliflower florets, ensuring florets are thoroughly coated
4. Pour in coconut milk and bring to a simmer
5. Cover and cook for 20-25 min until cauliflower is tender
6. Season with salt and garnish with fresh cilantro

Tips:

- Serve with basmati rice or naan bread for a complete meal
- Consider adding a bit of chili powder or fresh green chilies for extra heat

Nutritional Values: Calories: 290, Fat: 22g, Carbs: 22g, Protein: 6g, Sugar: 8g

SAVORY MUSHROOM AND WALNUT PÂTÉ

Preparation Time: 15 min
Cooking Time: none
Mode of Cooking: Mixing
Servings: 8
Ingredients:

- 2 cups cremini mushrooms, finely chopped
- 1 cup toasted walnuts, finely ground
- 1/4 cup shallots, minced
- 2 cloves garlic, minced
- 2 Tbsp olive oil
- 1 Tbsp tamari
- 1 Tbsp thyme, fresh
- 1 tsp black pepper

- 1 Tbsp lemon juice
- Salt to taste

Directions:

1. Heat olive oil in a skillet over medium heat
2. Sauté shallots and garlic until softened
3. Add mushrooms and cook until all moisture evaporates and mushrooms are golden
4. Remove from heat and let cool slightly
5. In a food processor, combine sautéed mushrooms, ground walnuts, tamari, thyme, black pepper, and lemon juice
6. Process until smooth and creamy
7. Season with salt to taste

Tips:

- Enjoy spread on toasted whole grain bread or as a dip with raw vegetables
- Can be refrigerated in an airtight container for up to 5 days

Nutritional Values: Calories: 190, Fat: 18g, Carbs: 5g, Protein: 4g, Sugar: 1g

MUSHROOM AND LENTIL SHEPHERD'S PIE

Preparation Time: 25 min
Cooking Time: 45 min
Mode of Cooking: Baking
Servings: 6
Ingredients:

- 1 lb brown lentils, rinsed and drained
- 4 cups vegetable broth
- 1 lb cremini mushrooms, finely chopped
- 2 Tbsp olive oil
- 1 large onion, diced
- 2 carrots, peeled and diced
- 2 celery stalks, diced
- 2 garlic cloves, minced
- 2 tsp thyme leaves
- 1 Tbsp tomato paste
- 1/4 cup red wine (optional)
- 3 Tbsp all-purpose flour
- 2 cups mashed potatoes

- Salt and pepper to taste

Directions:

1. Preheat oven to 400°F (204°C)
2. In a pot, simmer lentils in vegetable broth until tender, about 25 min
3. Heat oil in a large pan, add onions, carrots, celery, garlic, and sauté until soft
4. Add mushrooms, thyme, and cook until mushrooms are golden
5. Stir in tomato paste, then red wine, cook off the alcohol, and sprinkle flour over the mixture to thicken
6. Combine mushroom mixture with cooked lentils and transfer to a baking dish
7. Top with mashed potatoes and smooth out the top
8. Bake for 20 min or until the top is starting to brown

Tips:

- Opt for a creamy potato topping by adding a bit of vegan butter to the mash
- This dish can be prepped in advance and refrigerated overnight before baking
- Perfect for freezing leftovers for a quick meal

Nutritional Values: Calories: 340, Fat: 5g, Carbs: 55g, Protein: 18g, Sugar: 6g

ROASTED BEET AND WILD RICE PILAF

Preparation Time: 20 min
Cooking Time: 45 min
Mode of Cooking: Roasting/Baking
Servings: 4
Ingredients:

- 1½ cups cooked wild rice
- 3 medium beets, peeled and diced
- 1 large onion, chopped
- 2 cloves garlic, minced
- 3 Tbsp extra virgin olive oil
- 2 tsp fresh thyme, chopped
- 4 cups vegetable broth

- Salt and pepper to taste
- ½ cup chopped walnuts
- ½ cup crumbled goat cheese
- ¼ cup parsley, chopped

Directions:

1. Preheat oven to 375°F (190°C)
2. In a roasting tray, mix beets, onion, garlic, and olive oil
3. Roast for 30 min until beets are tender
4. In a large bowl, combine roasted vegetables with cooked wild rice, broth, thyme, salt, and pepper
5. Transfer to a baking dish and bake for 15 min
6. Garnish with walnuts, goat cheese, and parsley before serving

Tips:

- Add orange zest for a refreshing twist
- Toast walnuts prior to garnishing for enhanced flavor

Nutritional Values: Calories: 350, Fat: 18g, Carbs: 40g, Protein: 10g, Sugar: 8g

CHAPTER 8: SNACKS AND SIDES

It's often the little things that keep us on track with our health goals, isn't it? When life gets hectic, as it inevitably does, it's the quick, nourishing snacks and delightful sides that can safeguard our journey towards wellness. These small bites are not merely a bridge between meals; they embody the subtle yet significant pillars that can stabilize and invigorate your anti-inflammatory diet.

Imagine coming home from a busy day, weary and on the brink of opting for something less wholesome. Here, the power of a well-thought-out snack or side dish truly shines, transforming your day's course with its vibrant array of flavors and nutrients. Whether it's a crisp, refreshing carrot stick dipped in a creamy, herb-infused avocado spread, or a side of roasted Brussels sprouts glistening with a drizzle of olive oil and garlic, each recipe is crafted to be as pleasing to the palate as it is beneficial to your body.

Moreover, the magic of these recipes stretches beyond their immediate pleasure and convenience. Each serves as a stepping stone to more consistent eating habits. They're not just gaps fillers but pivotal components that add rhythm and enjoyment to your daily nutrition intake, making the wholesome choice an easy and obvious one.

In this chapter, we journey through a collection of snacks and sides that promise to be both comforting and inspiring. From veggie chips sprinkled with anti-inflammatory spices to sides that turn an ordinary meal into a feast of colors and flavors, these recipes are designed to be straightforward yet spectacular. They require minimal prep time but deliver maximum flavor and health benefits.

Let's embrace these small wonders and recognize their crucial role in our dietary choices. Here's to finding joy in the little things and turning every bite into an opportunity for health and healing. Dive into these pages filled with recipes tailored to energize you from one meal to the next, transforming your snack times into powerful, inflammation-fighting delights.

QUICK AND HEALTHY SNACKS

SPICY CHICKPEA POPCORN

Preparation Time: 5 min
Cooking Time: none
Mode of Cooking: No Cooking
Servings: 4

Ingredients:

- 1 can chickpeas, drained and dried
- 1 Tbsp olive oil
- 1 tsp smoked paprika
- 1/2 tsp garlic powder
- 1/4 tsp cayenne pepper
- 1/2 tsp sea salt

Directions:

1. Toss chickpeas with olive oil and all spices in a bowl until evenly coated
2. Spread on a baking sheet and let air dry for a few hours until crunchy

Tips:

- Add a teaspoon of nutritional yeast for a cheesy flavor
- Store in an airtight container to maintain crunchiness

Nutritional Values: Calories: 134, Fat: 5g, Carbs: 18g, Protein: 6g, Sugar: 3g

AVOCADO LIME RICE CAKES

Preparation Time: 10 min
Cooking Time: none
Mode of Cooking: No Cooking
Servings: 2
Ingredients:

- 2 plain rice cakes
- 1 ripe avocado, mashed
- Juice of 1 lime
- Pinch of chili flakes
- Salt and pepper to taste
- 1 Tbsp chopped cilantro

Directions:

1. Spread mashed avocado on rice cakes
2. Sprinkle with lime juice, chili flakes, salt, and pepper
3. Garnish with chopped cilantro

Tips:

- Experiment with different types of rice cakes for variety
- A drizzle of sriracha adds a nice heat

Nutritional Values: Calories: 190, Fat: 9g, Carbs: 21g, Protein: 3g, Sugar: 1g

ROSEMARY CITRUS OLIVES

Preparation Time: 15 min
Cooking Time: none
Mode of Cooking: No Cooking
Servings: 3
Ingredients:

- 1 cup mixed olives
- 1 Tbsp fresh rosemary, chopped

- Zest of 1 lemon
- 2 cloves garlic, minced
- 1 Tbsp olive oil
- 1/2 Tsp cracked black pepper

Directions:

1. Combine all ingredients in a bowl, mixing well to coat olives thoroughly
2. Let marinate for at least 1 hr before serving, stirring occasionally

Tips:

- Serve with wooden picks for easy eating
- Can be stored in the refrigerator for up to a week

Nutritional Values: Calories: 175, Fat: 18g, Carbs: 3g, Protein: 1g, Sugar: 0g

BEETROOT WALNUT DIP

Preparation Time: 10 min
Cooking Time: none
Mode of Cooking: No Cooking
Servings: 5
Ingredients:

- 2 medium-sized cooked beetroots, peeled and chopped
- 1/2 cup walnuts, toasted
- 1 garlic clove
- 2 Tbsp tahini
- 2 Tbsp lemon juice
- Salt and pepper to taste
- 1/4 tsp cumin

Directions:

1. Blend all ingredients in a food processor until smooth
2. Adjust seasoning to taste
3. Chill before serving

Tips:

- Pair with vegetable sticks or whole-grain crackers for a healthy snack

- Add a spoonful of Greek yogurt for a creamier texture

Nutritional Values: Calories: 123, Fat: 9g, Carbs: 8g, Protein: 3g, Sugar: 2g

CURRIED COCONUT CASHEWS

Preparation Time: 10 min
Cooking Time: 15 min
Mode of Cooking: Baking
Servings: 6
Ingredients:

- 2 cups cashews
- 1 Tbsp coconut oil, melted
- 1 Tbsp curry powder
- 1 tsp turmeric
- 1/2 tsp salt
- 1/4 cup shredded coconut

Directions:

1. Toss cashews with coconut oil, curry powder, turmeric, and salt
2. Spread on a baking sheet and bake at 350°F (175°C) for 15 min, stirring occasionally
3. Sprinkle with shredded coconut in the last 5 min of baking

Tips:

- Let cool completely before serving to enhance flavor development
- Store in an airtight container to preserve freshness

Nutritional Values: Calories: 255, Fat: 21g, Carbs: 15g, Protein: 7g, Sugar: 2g

SPIRULINA POPCORN DELIGHT

Preparation Time: 5 min
Cooking Time: none
Mode of Cooking: No Cooking
Servings: 4
Ingredients:

- ¼ C. popcorn kernels, air-popped
- 1 Tbsp coconut oil, melted
- 1 tsp spirulina powder
- ½ tsp garlic powder
- ¼ tsp cayenne pepper
- Salt to taste

Directions:

1. Place air-popped popcorn in a large bowl
2. Drizzle with melted coconut oil and toss to coat
3. Sprinkle spirulina, garlic powder, cayenne pepper, and salt over popcorn and toss again until evenly coated

Tips:

- Try using nutritional yeast for a cheesy flavor without the dairy
- Keep in an airtight container to maintain crunchiness

Nutritional Values: Calories: 80, Fat: 5g, Carbs: 9g, Protein: 2g, Sugar: 0g

TASTY SIDES

ROASTED TURMERIC CAULIFLOWER STEAKS

Preparation Time: 15 min
Cooking Time: 25 min
Mode of Cooking: Roasting
Servings: 4
Ingredients:

- 1 large head cauliflower, sliced into 4 steaks
- 2 Tbsp olive oil
- 1 tsp turmeric
- 1 tsp garlic powder
- 1/2 tsp smoked paprika
- Salt and black pepper to taste
- Fresh parsley, chopped for garnish

Directions:

1. Preheat oven to 400°F (200°C)

2. In a small bowl, mix olive oil, turmeric, garlic powder, smoked paprika, salt, and black pepper

3. Brush each cauliflower steak with the oil and spice mixture on both sides

4. Place on a baking sheet and roast in the oven, flipping halfway through, until golden and tender

Tips:

- Serve with a sprinkle of fresh parsley for a refreshing touch

- To ensure even cooking, slice cauliflower steaks of equal thickness

Nutritional Values: Calories: 107, Fat: 7g, Carbs: 10g, Protein: 4g, Sugar: 3g

SPIRALIZED BEET AND CARROT SALAD

Preparation Time: 20 min
Cooking Time: none
Mode of Cooking: No Cooking
Servings: 4
Ingredients:

- 3 large beets, peeled and spiralized
- 2 large carrots, peeled and spiralized
- 1/4 cup fresh lemon juice
- 2 Tbsp extra-virgin olive oil
- 1 Tbsp honey
- 2 tsp apple cider vinegar
- 1/4 cup fresh parsley, finely chopped
- Salt and black pepper to taste

Directions:

1. In a large bowl, combine spiralized beets and carrots

2. In a separate small bowl, whisk together lemon juice, olive oil, honey, and apple cider vinegar

3. Pour dressing over the spiralized vegetables and toss to coat thoroughly

4. Season with salt and pepper and garnish with chopped parsley

Tips:

- Add crumbled feta or goat cheese for a creamy texture and extra flavor

- This salad can be stored in the refrigerator for up to two days without losing its crunch

Nutritional Values: Calories: 136, Fat: 7g, Carbs: 18g, Protein: 2g, Sugar: 14g

GARLIC THYME MUSHROOMS

Preparation Time: 10 min
Cooking Time: 15 min
Mode of Cooking: Sautéing
Servings: 4
Ingredients:

- 2 Tbsp olive oil
- 1 lb mushrooms, cleaned and sliced
- 3 cloves garlic, minced
- 1 tsp dried thyme
- Salt and black pepper to taste
- 2 Tbsp fresh parsley, chopped for garnish

Directions:

1. Heat olive oil in a large skillet over medium heat

2. Add garlic and sauté until fragrant, about 1 minute

3. Add the mushrooms and thyme, season with salt and pepper, and sauté until mushrooms are golden and tender, about 15 minutes

4. Garnish with fresh parsley before serving

Tips:

- For a richer taste, finish the mushrooms with a splash of white wine before the final 2 minutes of sautéing

- Mushrooms release water while cooking; let this water evaporate to allow mushrooms to brown nicely

Nutritional Values: Calories: 98, Fat: 7g, Carbs: 8g, Protein: 3g, Sugar: 2g

ZESTY QUINOA AND BLACK BEAN SALAD

Preparation Time: 15 min
Cooking Time: 20 min
Mode of Cooking: Boiling
Servings: 6
Ingredients:

- 1 cup quinoa, rinsed
- 2 cups water
- 1 can black beans, rinsed and drained
- 1 red bell pepper, chopped
- 1/4 cup red onion, finely chopped
- 1/4 cup coriander, chopped
- 1 lime, juiced
- 1 Tbsp olive oil
- 1 tsp cumin
- Salt and black pepper to taste

Directions:

1. In a saucepan, bring water to a boil and add quinoa, reduce heat and simmer covered until all water is absorbed and quinoa is tender, about 15 min
2. Allow quinoa to cool slightly
3. In a large bowl, combine cooled quinoa, black beans, bell pepper, onion, and coriander
4. In a small bowl, mix lime juice, olive oil, and cumin to create the dressing
5. Pour dressing over the salad, mix well and season with salt and pepper

Tips:

- Chill before serving to enhance flavors
- Customize by adding diced avocado or cherry tomatoes for a fresh, summery twist

Nutritional Values: Calories: 215, Fat: 5g, Carbs: 35g, Protein: 8g, Sugar: 2g

BAKED SWEET POTATO WEDGES

Preparation Time: 10 min
Cooking Time: 35 min
Mode of Cooking: Baking
Servings: 4

Ingredients:

- 3 large sweet potatoes, cut into wedges
- 2 Tbsp olive oil
- 1 tsp smoked paprika
- 1/2 tsp garlic powder
- 1/2 tsp onion powder
- Salt and black pepper to taste

Directions:

1. Preheat oven to 425°F (220°C)
2. In a large bowl, toss sweet potato wedges with olive oil, smoked paprika, garlic powder, onion powder, salt, and black pepper
3. Arrange wedges in a single layer on a baking sheet
4. Bake in the oven until crisp and golden, about 35 minutes, turning halfway through

Tips:

- Serve with your favorite dip, such as avocado yogurt dip or classic ketchup
- Sprinkle with fresh rosemary or thyme after baking for an aromatic finish

Nutritional Values: Calories: 206, Fat: 7g, Carbs: 35g, Protein: 3g, Sugar: 7g

SPICY TURMERIC CAULIFLOWER STEAKS

Preparation Time: 15 min
Cooking Time: 25 min
Mode of Cooking: Roasting
Servings: 4
Ingredients:

- 1 large head cauliflower, sliced into 4 steaks
- 3 Tbsp olive oil
- 2 tsp ground turmeric
- 1 tsp paprika
- 1 tsp garlic powder
- 1/2 tsp black pepper
- 1 tsp sea salt
- 1/4 tsp cayenne pepper

Directions:

1. Preheat oven to 400°F (200°C)
2. In a small bowl, mix olive oil with turmeric, paprika, garlic powder, black pepper, sea salt, and cayenne pepper
3. Brush each cauliflower steak with the spice mixture
4. Place on a baking sheet and roast until golden and tender

Tips:

- Brush with additional olive oil halfway through for extra crispiness
- Serve with a drizzle of tahini for added creaminess and flavor

Nutritional Values: Calories: 150, Fat: 10g, Carbs: 15g, Protein: 4g, Sugar: 5g

DIPS AND SPREADS

GOLDEN TURMERIC HUMMUS

Preparation Time: 15 min.
Cooking Time: none
Mode of Cooking: No Cooking
Servings: 8
Ingredients:

- 1 can (15 oz.) chickpeas, rinsed and drained
- 1/4 cup tahini
- 3 Tbsp fresh lemon juice
- 2 Tbsp extra-virgin olive oil
- 1 tsp ground turmeric
- 1 clove garlic, minced
- 1/2 tsp cumin
- Salt to taste
- Water as needed for desired consistency

Directions:

1. Combine chickpeas, tahini, lemon juice, olive oil, turmeric, garlic, and cumin in a food processor

2. Process until smooth, adding water a little at a time to reach the desired consistency
3. Season with salt and adjust flavors to taste

Tips:

- Add a pinch of black pepper to enhance turmeric absorption
- Garnish with a sprinkle of paprika or a drizzle of olive oil for extra flavor
- Pair with fresh vegetables or whole-grain crackers for a healthy snack

Nutritional Values: Calories: 138, Fat: 8g, Carbs: 12g, Protein: 4g, Sugar: 2g

BEETROOT AND WALNUT DIP

Preparation Time: 20 min.
Cooking Time: none
Mode of Cooking: No Cooking
Servings: 6
Ingredients:

- 2 medium beetroots, cooked and peeled
- 1 cup walnuts, toasted
- 1 clove garlic
- 2 Tbsp tahini
- 1 Tbsp balsamic vinegar
- Salt and pepper to taste
- 1/4 cup extra-virgin olive oil

Directions:

1. Blend cooked beetroots, walnuts, garlic, tahini, and balsamic vinegar in a food processor until smooth
2. With the processor running, slowly add olive oil until fully incorporated
3. Season with salt and pepper to taste

Tips:

- Serve chilled or at room temperature for the best flavor
- Toasting walnuts before blending enhances their nutty essence
- For a creamy texture, add a dollop of Greek yogurt

Nutritional Values: Calories: 204, Fat: 18g, Carbs: 8g, Protein: 4g, Sugar: 4g

SPICY AVOCADO YOGURT DIP

Preparation Time: 10 min.
Cooking Time: none
Mode of Cooking: No Cooking
Servings: 4
Ingredients:

- 1 ripe avocado
- 1/2 cup Greek yogurt
- 1 Tbsp lime juice
- 1/2 tsp chili powder
- 1/4 tsp garlic powder
- Salt to taste
- Fresh cilantro, chopped for garnish

Directions:

1. Mash the avocado in a bowl
2. Mix in Greek yogurt, lime juice, chili powder, and garlic powder until well blended
3. Season with salt and garnish with fresh cilantro

Tips:

- For extra kick, add a pinch of cayenne pepper
- Keep the avocado seed in the bowl until serving to prevent browning

Nutritional Values: Calories: 98, Fat: 7g, Carbs: 6g, Protein: 2g, Sugar: 2g

AVOCADO AND WHITE BEAN SPREAD

Preparation Time: 10 min
Cooking Time: none
Mode of Cooking: No Cooking
Servings: 6
Ingredients:

- 1 ripe avocado, peeled and pitted
- 1 can (15 oz.) white beans, drained and rinsed
- 1 clove garlic, minced
- Juice of 1 lime
- 1 Tbsp chopped cilantro

- 1 Tbsp olive oil
- Salt and chili flakes to taste

Directions:

1. Blend avocado, white beans, garlic, lime juice, cilantro, and olive oil in a food processor until smooth
2. Season with salt and chili flakes to taste
3. Serve immediately or chill

Tips:

- Add a spoonful of Greek yogurt for a creamier texture
- Sprinkle some toasted pumpkin seeds on top for a crunchy finish
- Excellent spread on toasted whole-grain bread or as a dip with tortilla chips

Nutritional Values: Calories: 130, Fat: 7g, Carbs: 12g, Protein: 4g, Sugar: 1g

ROASTED BEET AND YOGURT DIP

Preparation Time: 15 min
Cooking Time: 45 min
Mode of Cooking: Roasting
Servings: 4
Ingredients:

- 2 medium beets, peeled and diced
- 1 cup Greek yogurt
- 1 Tbsp olive oil
- 2 tsp lemon juice
- 1 clove garlic, minced
- Salt and pepper to taste
- Fresh dill for garnish

Directions:

1. Preheat oven to 400°F (200°C)
2. Toss beets with olive oil, salt, and pepper and spread on a baking sheet
3. Roast until tender, about 45 min
4. Allow to cool slightly then blend roasted beets with Greek yogurt, lemon juice, and garlic in a food processor until smooth

5. Chill before serving

Tips:

- Garnish with chopped fresh dill and a few drops of olive oil
- Serve as a colorful side with grilled chicken or fish, or as a vegetable dip

Nutritional Values: Calories: 89, Fat: 3g, Carbs: 12g, Protein: 5g, Sugar: 9g

SPICY CARROT HARISSA SPREAD

Preparation Time: 20 min
Cooking Time: 30 min
Mode of Cooking: Roasting
Servings: 5
Ingredients:

- 5 large carrots, peeled and chopped
- 3 Tbsp olive oil
- 2 tsp harissa paste
- Juice of 1 lemon
- 1 tsp honey
- Salt to taste
- 2 Tbsp chopped pistachios for garnish

Directions:

1. Preheat oven to 375°F (190°C)
2. Toss chopped carrots with 2 Tbsp olive oil and roast until soft, about 30 min
3. Blend roasted carrots, remaining olive oil, harissa paste, lemon juice, honey, and salt in a food processor until smooth
4. Check seasoning and adjust if necessary

Tips:

- Sprinkle chopped pistachios before serving to add a nutty texture
- Can be spread on sandwiches or served with pita chips for a flavorful snack
- Keep refrigerated in a sealed container

Nutritional Values: Calories: 98, Fat: 7g, Carbs: 9g, Protein: 1g, Sugar: 5g

CHAPTER 9: DESSERTS

Welcome to the delightful world of desserts—where indulgence meets wellness. You may wonder, "Can desserts really align with an anti-inflammatory lifestyle?" The answer is a resounding "Yes!" This chapter is designed not just to satisfy your sweet tooth but to enhance your health without a pinch of guilt.

Imagine biting into a decadent, melt-in-your-mouth chocolate cake infused with pure, dark cocoa and sweetened naturally with ripe bananas and a hint of pure maple syrup. Or picture a sunny Sunday afternoon, enjoying a bowl of fresh berry sorbet, each spoonful bursting with antioxidant-rich berries and a zesty hint of fresh mint. Here, desserts aren't just treats; they're vibrant, full of life, and crafted with ingredients that align with our anti-inflammatory goals.

The journey through anti-inflammatory eating doesn't stop at savory meals; it extends gloriously into these sweet endings. With careful selection of ingredients, each recipe here is carefully balanced to ensure that inflammation is curtailed, not provoked. You will find options free from refined sugars and dairy, rich in nutrients, and full of natural flavors that speak to the soul of any dessert lover.

Each recipe has been tested and loved, designed not only to ease your body's inflammatory responses but also to bring joy and celebration to your table. These desserts are perfect for sharing with family and friends, proving that a healthful diet can indeed include delectable pleasures.

So, allow yourself the freedom to explore and enjoy. Whether you're concluding a hearty meal or simply need a little afternoon pick-me-up, these desserts offer a perfect, guilt-free capstone. Here's to finding sweetness in life, energized by foods that love us back in every bite.

SWEET TREATS WITH BENEFITS

GOLDEN TURMERIC CASHEW BARS WITH DATE CARAMEL

Preparation Time: 15 min
Cooking Time: none
Mode of Cooking: No Cooking
Servings: 16

Ingredients:

- 1½ C. raw cashews
- ½ C. shredded coconut, unsweetened
- ⅓ C. oat flour
- 2 Tbsp golden flaxseed meal
- 1 Tbsp ground turmeric
- ¼ tsp black pepper
- ⅓ C. coconut oil, melted
- ¼ C. maple syrup
- For the Date Caramel: 1 C. Medjool dates, pitted and soaked in warm water for 30 min
- ¼ C. almond milk
- 1 tsp vanilla extract
- Pinch of salt

Directions:

1. Combine cashews, coconut, oat flour, flaxseed meal, turmeric, and black pepper in a food processor and pulse to mix

2. Add melted coconut oil and maple syrup, process until mixture sticks together
3. Press firmly into a lined 8x8 inch pan
4. For the date caramel: Drain dates and blend with almond milk, vanilla, and salt until smooth
5. Spread caramel over the base layer, chill in the fridge for at least 2 hrs to set

Tips:

- Store bars in the fridge for up to 1 week for optimal freshness
- For a firmer caramel topping, freeze for an hour before serving

Nutritional Values: Calories: 230, Fat: 14g, Carbs: 25g, Protein: 5g, Sugar: 14g

LAVENDER INFUSED CHIA PUDDING

Preparation Time: 10 min
Cooking Time: 4 hr chilling
Mode of Cooking: Refrigerator
Servings: 8
Ingredients:

- 2 C. unsweetened almond milk
- ½ C. chia seeds
- 3 Tbsp raw honey or agave nectar
- 1 Tbsp culinary lavender
- ½ tsp vanilla extract
- Fresh berries for topping

Directions:

1. Combine almond milk, chia seeds, honey, lavender, and vanilla in a bowl and whisk thoroughly
2. Cover the mixture and refrigerate for at least 4 hr or overnight to allow chia seeds to swell and pudding to thicken
3. Serve topped with fresh berries

Tips:

- Strain lavender after whisking if preferred for a smoother texture

- Adjust sweetness by adding more honey or agave as per taste

Nutritional Values: Calories: 130, Fat: 7g, Carbs: 15g, Protein: 3g, Sugar: 8g

BEETROOT AND CHOCOLATE BLISS BALLS

Preparation Time: 20 min
Cooking Time: none
Mode of Cooking: No Cooking
Servings: 20
Ingredients:

- 1 C. raw beetroot, finely grated and excess juice squeezed out
- 1 C. walnuts
- ½ C. rolled oats
- ¼ C. raw cacao powder
- ⅓ C. dates, pitted
- 2 Tbsp chia seeds
- 1 tsp vanilla extract
- Pinch of salt
- Desiccated coconut or cocoa powder for rolling

Directions:

1. In a food processor, combine all ingredients except for rolling material and pulse until mixture forms a sticky dough
2. Scoop tablespoon-sized amounts and roll into balls
3. Roll the balls in desiccated coconut or cocoa powder to coat

Tips:

- Keep refrigerated in an airtight container to maintain freshness
- Can be frozen for up to one month for longer storage

Nutritional Values: Calories: 90, Fat: 5g, Carbs: 10g, Protein: 2g, Sugar: 5g

PEAR AND GINGER SORBET

Preparation Time: 15 min
Cooking Time: 4 hr freezing
Mode of Cooking: Freezer
Servings: 6
Ingredients:

- 4 ripe pears, peeled and cored
- ⅓ C. fresh ginger, minced
- Juice of 1 lemon
- ¼ C. honey
- 1 C. water

Directions:

1. In a saucepan over medium heat, combine water, ginger and honey, stirring until honey dissolves
2. Remove from heat, add lemon juice and let cool
3. Puree pears in a blender and mix with cooled ginger syrup
4. Pour mixture into an ice cream maker and churn according to manufacturer's instructions, then freeze until firm

Tips:

- Serve with a sprinkle of grated fresh ginger on top for extra zing
- No ice cream maker? Freeze mixture in a shallow pan and scrape every 30 min to fluff

Nutritional Values: Calories: 120, Fat: 0g, Carbs: 31g, Protein: 0.5g, Sugar: 28g

AVOCADO LIME CHEESECAKE

Preparation Time: 20 min
Cooking Time: 3 hr chilling
Mode of Cooking: Refrigerator
Servings: 8
Ingredients:

- For the crust: 1 C. almonds
- 1 C. Medjool dates, pitted
- ½ C. desiccated coconut
- For the filling: 3 ripe avocados
- Juice and zest of 2 limes
- ⅓ C. coconut cream
- ¼ C. honey
- 2 tsp vanilla extract

Directions:

1. To make the crust, pulse almonds, dates, and coconut in a food processor until a crumbly mixture forms, press firmly into the base of a 9-inch springform pan and chill
2. For the filling, blend avocados, lime juice and zest, coconut cream, honey, and vanilla until smooth and creamy
3. Pour the filling over the crust and refrigerate for at least 3 hr or until set

Tips:

- If the lime flavor is too intense, adjust by adding a bit more honey
- Decorate with thin lime slices or coconut flakes before serving for an extra elegant touch

Nutritional Values: Calories: 330, Fat: 25g, Carbs: 29g, Protein: 4g, Sugar: 18g

CACAO AVOCADO MOUSSE

Preparation Time: 15 min
Cooking Time: none
Mode of Cooking: No Cooking
Servings: 4
Ingredients:

- 1 ripe avocado, pitted and scooped
- ¼ C. raw cacao powder
- 3 Tbsp pure maple syrup
- 1 tsp pure vanilla extract
- Pinch of sea salt
- ½ C. chilled coconut cream

Directions:

1. Blend avocado, cacao powder, maple syrup, vanilla extract, and sea salt until smooth in a food processor

2. Add coconut cream and blend until creamy and smooth
3. Chill in the refrigerator for at least 1 hr before serving

Tips:

- Serve with fresh raspberries for added flavor and a pop of color
- Use high-quality cacao for a richer taste and additional antioxidants

Nutritional Values: Calories: 289, Fat: 22g, Carbs: 24g, Protein: 3g, Sugar: 12g

LIGHT AND REFRESHING OPTIONS

CHILLED MATCHA LIME CHEESECAKE

Preparation Time: 20 min
Cooking Time: none
Mode of Cooking: No Cooking
Servings: 8
Ingredients:

- 1 ½ cups almond flour
- ⅓ cup coconut oil, melted
- 2 Tbsp erythritol
- 1 pinch sea salt
- 2 cups raw cashews, soaked overnight and drained
- ⅔ cup canned coconut milk
- ½ cup lime juice, freshly squeezed
- ¼ cup honey
- 2 Tbsp matcha green tea powder

Directions:

1. Mix almond flour, coconut oil, erythritol, and salt until well combined and press into the base of a springform pan to form a crust
2. Blend cashews, coconut milk, lime juice, honey, and matcha until smooth and creamy
3. Pour over the crust and smooth the top
4. Refrigerate overnight or until set

Tips:

- Use high-quality matcha for best flavor
- If too thick, adjust the consistency of the filling with a bit more coconut milk
- Decorate with lime zest or thinly sliced lime rounds before serving

Nutritional Values: Calories: 410, Fat: 32g, Carbs: 26g, Protein: 8g, Sugar: 12g

FROZEN BLUEBERRY YOGURT BARS

Preparation Time: 15 min
Cooking Time: 4 hr
Mode of Cooking: Freezing
Servings: 10
Ingredients:

- 2 cups Greek yogurt, unsweetened
- 1 cup blueberries, fresh
- ¼ cup honey
- 1 Tbsp lemon zest
- 2 Tbsp chia seeds

Directions:

1. Mix Greek yogurt with honey, lemon zest, and chia seeds until thoroughly combined
2. Gently fold in blueberries
3. Spread the mixture into a parchment-lined baking tray
4. Freeze until solid, approximately 4 hours
5. Cut into bars

Tips:

- Incorporate a mix of berries for a colorful variant
- Slice bars while partially thawed for easier cutting
- Drizzle with dark chocolate for a decadent touch

Nutritional Values: Calories: 90, Fat: 1g, Carbs: 13g, Protein: 6g, Sugar: 10g

POMEGRANATE PISTACHIO MOUSSE

Preparation Time: 15 min
Cooking Time: 1 hr
Mode of Cooking: Chilling
Servings: 6
Ingredients:

- 1 ½ cups chilled coconut cream
- ⅓ cup pomegranate juice, fresh
- ¼ cup raw honey
- ½ cup pistachios, shelled and chopped
- 1 tsp vanilla extract

Directions:

1. Whip chilled coconut cream with pomegranate juice, honey, and vanilla extract until light and fluffy
2. Fold in most of the chopped pistachios, reserving some for topping
3. Spoon into serving dishes and chill for about 1 hour

Tips:

- Serve chilled garnished with reserved pistachios and pomegranate arils
- Adjust sweetness by varying the amount of honey based on your preference
- Ensure coconut cream is very cold before whipping to achieve the best texture

Nutritional Values: Calories: 300, Fat: 25g, Carbs: 18g, Protein: 4g, Sugar: 12g

COCONUT WATER AND FRUIT JELLY

Preparation Time: 10 min
Cooking Time: 3 hr
Mode of Cooking: Chilling
Servings: 8
Ingredients:

- 2 cups coconut water
- 3 Tbsp agar-agar flakes
- ½ cup mixed fruit (kiwi, berries, mango), finely chopped
- 2 Tbsp honey
- 1 tsp lime juice

Directions:

1. Heat coconut water until hot but not boiling and dissolve agar-agar flakes in it
2. Remove from heat and stir in honey and lime juice
3. Let the mixture cool slightly before adding the chopped fruit
4. Pour into molds or a shallow dish and refrigerate until set, about 3 hours

Tips:

- Use silicon molds for easy removal of the jelly shapes
- Adjust the amount of honey according to your desired sweetness level
- Experiment with different fruit combinations for variety

Nutritional Values: Calories: 50, Fat: 0g, Carbs: 11g, Protein: 0g, Sugar: 9g

RASPBERRY MINT SORBET

Preparation Time: 10 min
Cooking Time: 2 hr
Mode of Cooking: Freezing
Servings: 8
Ingredients:

- 3 cups raspberries, fresh
- ¼ cup mint leaves, fresh
- ½ cup water
- ⅔ cup erythritol
- 1 Tbsp lemon juice

Directions:

1. Blend raspberries, mint leaves, water, erythritol, and lemon juice until smooth
2. Strain the mixture through a fine sieve to remove seeds
3. Freeze in an ice cream maker according to the manufacturer's instructions, about 30-40 minutes, then transfer to a container and freeze for at least 2 hours to firm up

Tips:

- Opt for organic raspberries for a richer taste and natural sweetness
- Enhance the mint flavor by adding a few extra mint leaves during blending
- Serve with a sprig of fresh mint as a refreshing garnish

Nutritional Values: Calories: 70, Fat: 0.5g, Carbs: 18g, Protein: 1g, Sugar: 15g

CHILLED HONEYDEW CUCUMBER SOUP

Preparation Time: 15 min
Cooking Time: none
Mode of Cooking: No Cooking
Servings: 4
Ingredients:

- 1 medium honeydew melon, peeled and cubed
- 1 large cucumber, peeled and chopped
- 1 cup coconut water
- 2 Tbsp fresh lime juice
- 1 Tbsp fresh mint, chopped
- 1/4 tsp salt
- 1/4 cup plain yogurt for garnish
- Mint leaves for garnish

Directions:

1. Blend honeydew, cucumber, coconut water, lime juice, chopped mint, and salt until smooth
2. Pour into bowls
3. Garnish with a dollop of yogurt and mint leaves

Tips:

- Serve chilled for a refreshing finish
- Blend until absolutely smooth for the best texture

Nutritional Values: Calories: 120, Fat: 0.5g, Carbs: 25g, Protein: 2g, Sugar: 20g

INDULGENT DESSERTS

LAVENDER HONEY CHEESECAKE

Preparation Time: 20 min
Cooking Time: 45 min
Mode of Cooking: Baking
Servings: 8
Ingredients:

- 1½ cups almond flour
- ¼ cup coconut oil, melted
- 2 Tbsp erythritol
- 3 cups cream cheese, softened
- 1 cup Greek yogurt
- ¾ cup raw honey
- 3 large eggs
- 2 Tbsp culinary lavender, finely ground
- 1 tsp vanilla extract

Directions:

1. Preheat oven to 325°F (163°C)
2. Combine almond flour, coconut oil, and erythritol to form the crust; press into the bottom of a springform pan and set aside
3. Beat cream cheese until smooth, then incorporate Greek yogurt, honey, eggs, lavender, and vanilla until creamy
4. Pour mixture over crust and bake until set, about 45 min
5. Cool and then chill overnight in refrigerator

Tips:

- Use culinary lavender for a subtle floral hint
- Pair with a light vanilla bean ice cream for an extra indulgence

Nutritional Values: Calories: 485, Fat: 39g, Carbs: 26g, Protein: 11g, Sugar: 18g

DARK CHOCOLATE AVOCADO TRUFFLES

Preparation Time: 15 min
Cooking Time: none
Mode of Cooking: Mixing
Servings: 20

Ingredients:

- 2 ripe avocados, mashed
- 1 cup dark cocoa powder
- ½ cup coconut sugar
- 1 tsp pure vanilla extract
- ¼ tsp sea salt
- ½ cup crushed pistachios for coating

Directions:

1. Mix mashed avocados, cocoa powder, coconut sugar, vanilla, and sea salt until smooth
2. Form into small balls and roll in crushed pistachios
3. Chill for 2 hrs until firm

Tips:

- Store in an airtight container in the fridge to maintain freshness
- Substitute pistachios with toasted almond flakes for a different flavor
- Roll truffles in cocoa powder instead for a classic finish

Nutritional Values: Calories: 120, Fat: 8g, Carbs: 10g, Protein: 2g, Sugar: 5g

SAFFRON PISTACHIO PANNA COTTA

Preparation Time: 10 min
Cooking Time: 4 hr chilling
Mode of Cooking: Chilling
Servings: 6
Ingredients:

- 2 cups heavy cream
- 1 cup whole milk
- 1 tsp saffron threads
- ⅓ cup sugar
- 1 Tbsp gelatin, powdered
- ¼ cup warm water
- ½ cup shelled pistachios, chopped
- Edible gold leaf for decoration

Directions:

1. Dissolve gelatin in warm water and set aside
2. Heat cream, milk, sugar, and saffron in a saucepan until just boiling; remove from heat
3. Stir in gelatin until fully dissolved
4. Pour into molds and refrigerate until set, about 4 hrs
5. Garnish with chopped pistachios and gold leaf before serving

Tips:

- Experiment with rose water for an extra aromatic experience
- Serve chilled to maintain the perfect consistency of the panna cotta

Nutritional Values: Calories: 310, Fat: 25g, Carbs: 18g, Protein: 5g, Sugar: 17g

MATCHA WHITE CHOCOLATE MOUSSE

Preparation Time: 20 min
Cooking Time: 2 hr chilling
Mode of Cooking: Whisking
Servings: 4
Ingredients:

- 3 Tbsp matcha green tea powder
- 1 cup white chocolate chips, melted
- 2 cups heavy cream
- ¼ cup sugar
- ½ tsp vanilla extract
- Fresh raspberries for topping

Directions:

1. Melt white chocolate chips gently and let cool slightly
2. Whisk heavy cream, sugar, and vanilla until soft peaks form
3. Gradually add matcha powder to the melted white chocolate, stirring continuously
4. Fold matcha chocolate mixture into the whipped cream gently
5. Spoon into dessert cups and chill for 2 hr
6. Top with fresh raspberries before serving

Tips:

- Add a pinch of salt to enhance the matcha flavor
- Decorate with mint leaves for a fresh look
- Serve in clear cups to show off the beautiful layers

Nutritional Values: Calories: 422, Fat: 32g, Carbs: 31g, Protein: 4g, Sugar: 29g

CARDAMOM ROSE RICE PUDDING

Preparation Time: 10 min
Cooking Time: 25 min
Mode of Cooking: Simmering
Servings: 6
Ingredients:

- 1 cup basmati rice, rinsed
- 4 cups almond milk
- ½ cup sugar
- 2 tsp cardamom, ground
- 1 Tbsp rose water
- Pistachios, chopped, and dried rose petals for garnish

Directions:

1. Combine rice, almond milk, sugar, and cardamom in a large saucepan and bring to a simmer, stirring frequently
2. Reduce heat and continue to simmer until rice is tender and milk is mostly absorbed, about 25 min
3. Stir in rose water and remove from heat
4. Serve warm or chilled, garnished with chopped pistachios and rose petals

Tips:

- Experiment with different types of milk for varying creaminess
- Garnish with a sprinkle of cinnamon for an added spice kick

Nutritional Values: Calories: 210, Fat: 3g, Carbs: 42g, Protein: 5g, Sugar: 18g

SPICED COCONUT RICE PUDDING

Preparation Time: 10 min
Cooking Time: 35 min
Mode of Cooking: Simmering
Servings: 6
Ingredients:

- 1 cup Arborio rice
- 4 cups light coconut milk
- 1/2 cup coconut sugar
- 1 vanilla bean, split and scraped
- 1 tsp ground cinnamon
- 1/4 tsp grated nutmeg
- 1/2 cup raisins

Directions:

1. Combine Arborio rice and light coconut milk in a saucepan over medium heat
2. Add coconut sugar, vanilla bean (both the seeds and pod), cinnamon, and nutmeg and bring to a simmer
3. Reduce heat to low and cook, stirring occasionally, until the rice is tender and the mixture is creamy, about 35 min
4. Remove from heat and stir in raisins

Tips:

- Serve warm or chilled, garnished with a sprinkle of cinnamon
- Leftovers can be refreshed with a splash of additional coconut milk before reheating
- For a vegan variant, ensure that the coconut sugar is certified vegan

Nutritional Values: Calories: 275, Fat: 4g, Carbs: 55g, Protein: 5g, Sugar: 20g

CHAPTER 10: 30-DAY MEAL PLAN

Embark on a transformative 30-day journey where each meal is not merely about sustenance but about igniting change. Imagine each dish as a brushstroke on the vibrant canvas of your health, the colors emerging fuller and more vibrant with every passing day. This chapter is designed to provide you with a sequential meal plan that introduces the simplicity and delight of an anti-inflammatory lifestyle, one delicious meal at a time.

We begin under the gentle guidance of intention—a commitment to nourish not only your body but your spirit. Setting a course for wellness may feel daunting, reminiscent of a leap into unknown waters. However, remember, each step taken towards this goal is cushioned with knowledge, adorned with flavors, and linked with easy, actionable practices that fit right into your bustling life.

Throughout the upcoming weeks, you will explore an array of recipes formulated to foster convenience, flavor, and nutritional balance. Picture this: starting your days with smoothies blended with the fresh zest of anti-inflammatory fruits, and winding down your evenings with a warm, spice-bathed meal that assures rest and rejuvenation. Every week, promises a new theme, bringing closer the foods that cool inflammation and boost your vitality.

The power of transformation lies in persistence and the beauty of this meal plan lies in its gradual building of your lifestyle repertoire—no drastic changes, just steady, loving tweaks to your daily habits, curated to build momentum and sustain it. Week by week, as you pour over the planned recipes and integrate them into your daily rhythm, you will begin to notice subtle yet profound changes. These seemingly small victories—more energy, clearer skin, a calmer digestive system—are the whispers of your body thanking you.

By the time you turn the last page of this chapter, achieving your goals will not just be a possibility but a brightly colored reality. This 30-day meal plan isn't just a roadmap—it's a gateway to lifelong habits that celebrate the joy of healthy living. Let's take this step together, relishing each meal and cherishing each moment on this journey to a revitalized, energetic you.

WEEK 1: GETTING STARTED

WEEK 1	breakfast	snack	lunch	snack	dinner
Monday	Turmeric Quinoa Power Breakfast Bowl	Greek yogurt with honey	Quinoa and Black Bean Salad with Cilantro-Lime Dressing	Apple slices with almond butter	Tuscan Garlic Turmeric Chicken
Tuesday	Chia and Almond Overnight Oats	Carrot sticks with beetroot walnut dip	Smoked Turkey and Spinach Salad with Cranberry Vinaigrette	A small bowl of blueberries	Lemon Herb Roasted Chicken
Wednesday	Broccoli and Chickpea Breakfast Hash	A handful of mixed nuts	Chickpea and Roasted Vegetable Salad with Cumin Vinaigrette	Sliced bell peppers with guacamole	Ginger-Lime Baked Cod
Thursday	Mushroom and Goat Cheese Frittata	Cucumber slices with hummus	Avocado and Mango Salad with Citrus Dressing	Greek yogurt with fresh fruit	Moroccan Chicken Tagine
Friday	Savory Oatmeal with Shiitake Mushrooms and Spinach	A small bowl of mixed berries	Grilled Chicken and Quinoa Tabbouleh Salad	A small handful of walnuts	Quinoa and Black Bean Stuffed Peppers
Saturday	Apple Cinnamon Quinoa Bowl	Celery sticks with almond butter	Asian Tofu Salad with Sesame Ginger Dressing	Carrot sticks with tzatziki sauce	Spiced Lamb Tagine with Apricots and Almonds
Sunday	Green Tea Chia Pudding	A handful of almonds	Roasted Beet and Citrus Salad with Pistachio Dressing	A small apple	Mediterranean Salmon with Fennel and Olives

WEEK 2: BUILDING MOMENTUM

WEEK 2	breakfast	snack	lunch	snack	dinner
Monday	Spinach and Feta Breakfast Wraps	Greek yogurt with honey and nuts	Chickpea Tuna Salad with Avocado Dressing	Sliced bell peppers with hummus	Spicy Maple Dijon Glazed Chicken
Tuesday	Berry Quinoa Breakfast Bowl	A small bowl of strawberries	Grilled Chicken and Quinoa Tabbouleh Salad	A small bowl of mixed berries	Beef Rouladen with Pickle and Mustard Filling
Wednesday	Mushroom and Herb Omelet	Carrot sticks with hummus	Asian Tofu Salad with Sesame Ginger Dressing	Celery sticks with almond butter	Herbed Haddock en Papillote
Thursday	Chia and Coconut Yogurt Parfait	Apple slices with almond butter	Roasted Beet and Citrus Salad with Pistachio Dressing	A small handful of walnuts	Cauliflower Tikka Masala
Friday	Savory Oat Hash	A handful of mixed nuts	Quinoa and Black Bean Salad with Cilantro-Lime Dressing	Greek yogurt with fresh fruit	Miso Glazed Eggplant Steaks
Saturday	Almond Butter and Banana Open Sandwich	Cucumber slices with guacamole	Smoked Turkey and Spinach Salad with Cranberry Vinaigrette	Carrot sticks with tzatziki sauce	Pork Tenderloin with Plum Sauce
Sunday	Turmeric Quinoa Power Breakfast Bowl	A small handful of blueberries	Chickpea and Roasted Vegetable Salad with Cumin Vinaigrette	A small apple	Chili Garlic Shrimp Skewers

WEEK 3: STAYING CONSISTENT

WEEK 3	breakfast	snack	lunch	snack	dinner
Monday	Golden Turmeric Sunrise Smoothie	A small bowl of mixed berries	Rainbow Quinoa and Pomegranate Salad	A small bowl of strawberries	Moroccan Chicken Tagine
Tuesday	Spinach and Feta Breakfast Wrap	Cucumber slices with beetroot walnut dip	Watermelon and Feta Salad with Mint	Sliced bell peppers with guacamole	Lemon Herb Roasted Chicken
Wednesday	Savory Oatmeal with Shiitake Mushrooms and Spinach	Greek yogurt with honey	Asian Cucumber and Edamame Salad with Wasabi Vinaigrette	Celery sticks with almond butter	Ginger-Lime Baked Cod
Thursday	Green Tea Chia Pudding	A handful of almonds	Smoked Turkey and Spinach Salad with Cranberry Vinaigrette	Greek yogurt with fresh fruit	Cauliflower Tikka Masala
Friday	Broccoli and Chickpea Breakfast Hash	Apple slices with almond butter	Grilled Chicken and Quinoa Tabbouleh Salad	A small handful of mixed nuts	Miso Glazed Eggplant Steaks
Saturday	Mushroom and Goat Cheese Frittata	Carrot sticks with hummus	Chickpea Tuna Salad with Avocado Dressing	A small apple	Pork Tenderloin with Plum Sauce
Sunday	Apple Cinnamon Quinoa Bowl	A small handful of walnuts	Avocado and Mango Salad with Citrus Dressing	Carrot sticks with tzatziki sauce	Chili Garlic Shrimp Skewers

WEEK 4: ACHIEVING YOUR GOALS

WEEK 4	breakfast	snack	lunch	snack	dinner
Monday	Chia and Coconut Yogurt Delight	A small handful of mixed nuts	Asian Pear and Baby Spinach Salad with Gorgonzola	Greek yogurt with fresh fruit	Turmeric-Spiced Lamb Chops with Cilantro Gremolata
Tuesday	Mushroom and Herb Omelet	Greek yogurt with honey and nuts	Watermelon and Feta Salad with Mint	Celery sticks with almond butter	Seared Tuna and Arugula Salad
Wednesday	Spinach and Feta Breakfast Wrap	Carrot sticks with beetroot walnut dip	Grilled Chicken and Quinoa Tabbouleh Salad	A small handful of walnuts	Herbed Haddock en Papillote
Thursday	Almond Butter and Banana Open Sandwich	Cucumber slices with hummus	Chickpea and Roasted Vegetable Salad with Cumin Vinaigrette	Carrot sticks with tzatziki sauce	Spiced Lamb Tagine with Apricots and Almonds
Friday	Turmeric Quinoa Power Breakfast Bowl	A small bowl of strawberries	Avocado and Strawberry Quinoa Salad	A small apple	Quinoa and Black Bean Stuffed Peppers
Saturday	Chia and Almond Overnight Oats	Apple slices with almond butter	Quinoa and Black Bean Salad with Cilantro-Lime Dressing	Sliced bell peppers with guacamole	Moroccan Chicken Tagine
Sunday	Broccoli and Chickpea Breakfast Hash	A handful of almonds	Smoked Turkey and Spinach Salad with Cranberry Vinaigrette	A small bowl of mixed berries	Chili Garlic Shrimp Skewers

CHAPTER 11: TIPS FOR LONG-TERM SUCCESS

Embracing an anti-inflammatory lifestyle is a journey, not just a destination, and the true art lies in its sustainability. As we turn the page to the final chapter of our exploration together, I want us to focus on ensuring that you have the tools, knowledge, and inspiration to continue this path confidently and joyfully.

Imagine you've planted a garden in which the seeds of your knowledge about anti-inflammatory foods have sprouted into routines and recipes you now cherish. However, like any garden, the beauty and productivity of your efforts depend on consistent care and adaptation through changing seasons. This chapter is akin to learning how to tend to that garden through all climates, ensuring that it throws back flourishing returns year after year. Navigating long-term success involves more than sticking strictly to a diet; it encompasses a mindset shift and a lifestyle orientation that appreciates the ebbs and flows. It's about making informed, flexible choices that align with your body's needs and your family's tastes. The goal is to make this not just feasible but enjoyable—turning 'must do' into 'want to do.'

Let's discuss how to maintain the fiery enthusiasm you started with, even when the initial excitement of new flavors and dishes begins to normalize. I'll share strategies on how to adapt your palette to the rhythms of your life and the seasons, ensuring diversity and delight in your meals. We'll explore how to rekindle your motivation by revisiting your goals and celebrating your milestones, all while continuing to nourish your body in the most beneficial ways.

We'll also address the common barriers you may encounter over time—from the temptation of old eating habits to navigating social settings and dietary challenges. Understanding how to empower yourself with smart, spontaneous choices can make all the difference between a temporary diet and a lasting wellness lifestyle.

By the end of this chapter, you will be equipped not only with meal plans but with resilience and adaptability—key ingredients to nourishing not just your body, but also your soul, in the years to come. Let's celebrate each step forward, learning and growing as we go, making the anti-inflammatory diet a well-loved, lived-in element of your life.

MAINTAINING YOUR ANTI-INFLAMMATORY DIET

In the mosaic of our lives, maintaining an anti-inflammatory diet emerges as a consistent thread of gold that weaves through our daily routines, challenging yet overwhelmingly rewarding. As the weeks turn into months, and dramatic initial progress may plateau into subtler increments of wellness, the key to sustained success lies in embedding this healthful pattern deeply into the fabric of your existence.

Let's explore how the philosophies and practices of an anti-inflammatory life can transform from conscious efforts to intuitive aspects of your day-to-day living. We are looking beyond the boundaries of a 'diet' and into the realms of lifelong nutrition and wellness.

Embracing Flexibility Within Structure

When you first committed to an anti-inflammatory diet, structured meal plans and specific food lists were likely your guides; they illuminated the path. As time progresses, however, relying on rigid structures can become both impractical and stifling. Instead, imagine your diet as a jazz improvisation—a structured melody line, yet played with personal flair and spontaneous variations adapted to your current mood and social setting.

Achieving this composed flexibility means understanding the foundational principles of anti-inflammatory eating so thoroughly that you can make informed choices on the fly. It's about knowing which foods trigger inflammation and which soothe, without needing to consult a chart. Over time this knowledge becomes second nature, like knowing to bring an umbrella if the day is cloudy.

Creating a Supportive Environment

Your surroundings play an essential role in maintaining your dietary habits. From the pantry to the workplace lunchroom, to the dinner table at a friend's house, environments can encourage or dissuade our food choices. Begin by transforming your home environment: clear out pro-inflammatory foods and stock your kitchen with wholesome, beneficial ingredients. Make your environment a fortress of your commitment—a place where maintaining your anti-inflammatory lifestyle is as natural as breathing.

Moreover, social settings needn't be battlegrounds for sticking to your diet goals. Educate and involve your family and friends in your journey. When they understand why you've made these changes—and notice the health benefits you're reaping—they're more likely to support you and perhaps even join you in this lifestyle shift.

Harnessing the Power of Routine and Ritual

Once the novelty wears off, the danger is that boredom or complacency sets in. Counteract this by establishing routines and rituals around your meals and food preparation. Perhaps Sunday is your meal-prep day, or each morning starts with a soothing anti-inflammatory smoothie. These habits serve as anchors, ensuring that even on your busiest or toughest days, you have a framework to support you.

On the other hand, rituals imbue your mealtime with a sense of ceremony and mindfulness, which can elevate your dining experience and enhance your relationship with food. It could be as simple as taking a deep breath before you begin eating to fully engage your senses and express gratitude for the nourishment you are about to receive.

Listening to Your Body: Advanced Intuition

"Listen to your body" sounds like straightforward advice, but in practice, it is a skill honed over time. It involves deepening your awareness of how foods affect you—not just in the moment, but in the longer-term effects they have on your body and mind. Keeping a food journal can be immensely beneficial, especially in the stages where the diet still feels new and you're determining which tweaks work best for you.

This dialogue with your body can guide you in adapting your diet more creatively and personally. You notice what makes you feel energetic and what weighs you down, what soothes your digestion and what irritates it. This ongoing internal conversation ensures that your diet evolves with your changing health needs and life circumstances.

Celebrating and Recalibrating

Celebrating your successes, big and small, helps propel your journey forward. Acknowledge milestones like sustaining the diet for six months or when a specific inflammatory symptom improves. These celebrations can reinforce the value of your efforts and remind you why you embarked on this path.

Conversely, be equally prepared to recalibrate. If you encounter setbacks (and most people do), view them as opportunities to learn and adjust, not as reasons for guilt or discouragement. Revisit your goals and strategies, perhaps with the help of a nutritionist or a supportive community. Adjustments—whether they are changing up your food choices, tweaking meal timings, or addressing stress management—are all part of the journey's natural ebb and flow.

Sustaining the Spark: Education and Community

Lastly, your intellectual and communal engagements play a significant role in maintaining an anti and-inflammatory diet. Stay curious—read the latest research, follow thought leaders in the space, and experiment with new, anti-inflammatory ingredients and recipes. Engaging with a community—whether online or in person—can provide a wellspring of motivation, accountability, and support.

Through community, we find not just companionship but also a mirror reflecting our shared and individual journeys in wellness. Engage actively in support groups, cooking classes, or online forums. When challenges arise, these communal connections can offer solutions and solace, keeping you steadfast on your path.

In stitching these strategies into the narrative of your life, the anti-inflammatory diet transcends from a regimen to a rewarding, deeply ingrained way of life. It becomes less about what you can't have and more about all that you gain. Consider this journey a tapestry of well-being, woven with the threads of knowledge, support, and perseverance into a vibrant tableau of enduring health.

ADAPTING RECIPES FOR SEASONAL INGREDIENTS

Seasons change, and so do the colors and flavors on our plates. Embracing the seasonal rhythms of nature not only adds variety to our meals but also aligns our diet more closely with the environment, enhancing the nutritional value and freshness of what we eat. This deep connection between our health and the health of our planet illustrates a beautiful symmetry: as the Earth provides for us, we care for it in return by choosing sustainable, locally-sourced options.

The art of adapting recipes to incorporate seasonal ingredients involves both creativity and mindfulness, allowing us to stay committed to an anti-inflammatory diet while celebrating the diversity of nature's offerings. It is a dynamic way to maintain interest and excitement in your meal planning, all while upholding the principles of healthy, anti-inflammatory eating.

The Benefits of Seasonal Eating

Eating seasonally ensures that you are receiving the highest possible concentrations of nutrients. Produce that is picked when it's fully ripe contains more vitamins, minerals, and antioxidants. The journey from farm to table is shorter, reducing nutrient loss that often occurs during transportation over long distances. Additionally, seasonal produce tends to be less expensive and its purchase supports local farmers and economies, creating a symbiotic relationship between your health and your community.

Intuitive Connection with Nature's Cycles

To adapt your diet to seasonal changes, begin by fostering a closer relationship with the local food sources in your area. Visit farmers' markets, join a community-supported agriculture (CSA) program, or even start your own garden. These actions not only connect you more deeply with the source of your food but also help you naturally learn what grows when in your region.

As you become more attuned to the cycles of nature, you'll start to notice which foods make your body feel best at different times of the year. For example, the light, cool fruits of summer can be refreshing and hydrating during hot months, while the dense, rich root vegetables of winter can offer satisfying warmth and energy during colder times.

Adapting Your Favorite Recipes

The cornerstone of keeping your anti-inflammatory diet exciting and diverse is adaptability. Take your favorite recipes and think about how they might be modified to incorporate seasonal produce. Here are some general guidelines:

1. **Substitute with similarity**: Replace fruits and vegetables with others that have similar textures and cooking properties. For example, zucchini in the summer can be swapped for squash in the fall.

2. **Adjust cooking methods**: Summer might call for grilling and raw salads, while winter invites slow-cooked stews and roasts. These methods not only bring out the natural goodness of seasonal produce but also cater to our body's changing needs.
3. **Herbs and spices**: Seasonal changes can be complemented by adjusting the herbs and spices used in recipes. Cooling herbs like mint and cilantro are wonderful in the summer, while warming spices such as ginger and turmeric can be comforting in the winter.

Learning and Experimentation: Grow Your Culinary Skills

Each season brings its own set of challenges and opportunities for culinary creativity. Winter's squash can be daunting if you've never cooked it before, but mastering a few simple roasting techniques can open up a myriad of possibilities. Likewise, the abundance of summer tomatoes offers a chance to perfect your homemade salsa or pasta sauce.

Engage with other food enthusiasts, whether through online communities, cooking classes, or simply friends who love to cook. Sharing tips, challenges, and successes can make the process of adapting recipes less daunting and more enjoyable.

Mindful Eating through the Seasons

Part of adapting to seasonal ingredients is developing the habit of mindful eating. This practice involves paying close attention to the tastes, textures, and smells of your meals, as well as how they make you feel. In this way, seasonal eating can become a holistic sensory experience, deepening your connection to your food and to the moment.

Mindful eating also helps you tune into your body's responses to different foods. Over time, you may notice that your body craves certain types of produce at particular times of year—this is your internal wisdom aligning with the external environment. Trusting and honoring these cravings can enhance your physical and emotional well-being.

Continuous Learning and Adaptation

As you journey through the cycle of seasons, remember that each year brings its own lessons and revelations. What worked one summer might be different the next, due to changes in weather, availability, or your personal health needs. Stay flexible and open to change.

Keep a seasonal food diary as part of your exploration. Note what you tried, what you loved, and what you might do differently next time. This record can become a personal cookbook of sorts—one that evolves with you and your diet, year after year.

By embracing the fluidity of seasonal eating, you empower yourself to craft a sustainably healthy lifestyle that respects both your body and the planet. It transforms the act of eating from a mundane daily necessity into an engaging dialogue with the natural world, enriching your life and ensuring your long-term success on an anti-inflammatory diet.

STAYING MOTIVATED AND INSPIRED

The journey to wellness, particularly through the adoption of an anti-inflammatory diet, is much like following a winding path through a dense, enchanting forest. There are moments of awe and profound beauty, interspersed with inevitable obstacles and setbacks. One of the most crucial skills you can cultivate on this journey is the ability to stay motivated and inspired, even when the path seems obscured.

Understanding Motivation in Your Wellness Journey

Motivation is not a constant; it ebbs and flows with the tides of our lives. Recognizing this can significantly relieve the pressure you might feel to always be at peak inspiration and motivation. Just as your body requires different nutrients at different times, your mind requires varying types of motivation and inspiration.

There are two main types of motivation: intrinsic and extrinsic. Intrinsic motivation comes from within; it is driven by personal satisfaction and interest in the diet itself. Extrinsic motivation, however, is influenced by external factors, such as the desire to improve one's appearance or to receive praise from others. Understanding which type drives you most can help tailor your approach to staying motivated.

Drawing Inspiration from Personal Goals

Setting clear, achievable goals is the backbone of sustained motivation. Goals should be specific enough to be measurable yet flexible enough to evolve with your needs and circumstances. As you move further along your dietary journey, revisit and adjust your goals as necessary. This practice not only helps keep your objectives relevant and motivating but also provides a tangible sense of progress and achievement.

Finding Your Community

Humans are inherently social creatures, and finding a community of like-minded individuals can provide a substantial motivational boost. Community connections offer emotional support, provide accountability, and can even foster healthy competition. Whether online or in-person, look for groups focused on anti-inflammatory living, health and wellness, or general healthy eating. Sharing your experiences and learning from the experiences of others can be incredibly inspiring.

Celebrating Small Victories

In the long pursuit of wellness, it's easy to overlook the small victories that occur along the way. Acknowledging and celebrating these moments is vital for sustaining motivation. Did you choose a healthy snack over a less healthy option? Have you followed through with your planned meals for the week? These are successes worth recognizing. Celebrating these small milestones helps build confidence and reinforces the positive impact of your dietary choices.

Engaging With New Knowledge

Continuously educating yourself about the principles of anti-inflammatory nutrition can also renew your interest and commitment. The more you understand about how certain foods affect inflammation and your overall health, the more intriguing and engaging your dietary choices become. Books, articles, webinars, and workshops provide fresh insights and remind you of the importance and impact of your efforts.

Mindfulness and Reflection

Mindfulness practices can enhance your motivation by connecting you more deeply with the present moment and with the physical and emotional sensations associated with eating. Through mindful eating, you become acutely aware of the taste, texture, and effects of food, which can transform eating from a mundane task into a profound experience. Additionally, regular reflection through journaling can help you track your progress, understand your challenges, and maintain motivation by making abstract achievements concrete and visible.

Visualize Success

Visualization is a powerful tool for maintaining motivation. By creating a vivid mental image of yourself achieving your goals, you can inspire a deep emotional commitment to the daily choices that lead to these outcomes. Visualization not only boosts motivation but can also improve mental well-being and reduce stress levels, making the dietary journey more enjoyable and effective.

Integrating Rewards

Integrate rewards into your routine to make maintaining your anti-inflammatory diet more of a pleasure than a chore. These rewards should not counteract your progress but should complement it. Consider indulging in a massage after a month of sticking to your diet plan, or buying a new cookbook to expand your culinary skills. Rewards that enhance your lifestyle changes can reinforce positive behaviors while providing an enjoyable reprieve from routine.

Renewing Your Approach

Finally, don't be afraid to shake things up if your routine starts to feel stale. Experimenting with new recipes, changing your meal planning schedule, or trying a new fitness routine to complement your diet can all reinvigorate your enthusiasm. Change can be refreshing and can reignite the initial excitement you felt at the beginning of your health journey.

In weaving these strategies into the tapestry of your life, remember that motivation is deeply personal and what works for others may not work for you. Be patient, be persistent, and most importantly, be kind to yourself as you navigate the complexities of maintaining an inspired, motivated stance toward an anti-inflammatory lifestyle. With each small step, you are carving a path not just toward improved health, but toward a richer, more vibrant life.

APPENDIX

MEASUREMENT CONVERSION CHART

Volume Measurements

US Measurement	Metric Measurement
1 tsp (tsp)	5 milliliters (ml)
1 tbsp (tbsp)	15 milliliters (ml)
1 fluid ounce (fl oz)	30 milliliters (ml)
1 Cup	240 milliliters (ml)
1 pint (2 Cs)	470 milliliters (ml)
1 quart (4 Cs)	0.95 liters (L)
1 gallon (16 Cs)	3.8 liters (L)

Weight Measurements

US Measurement	Metric Measurement
1 ounce (oz)	28 grams (g)
1 pound (lb)	450 grams (g)
1 pound (lb)	0.45 kilograms (kg)

Length Measurements

US Measurement	Metric Measurement
1 inch (in)	2.54 centimeters (cm)
1 foot (ft)	30.48 centimeters (cm)
1 foot (ft)	0.3048 meters (m)
1 yard (yd)	0.9144 meters (m)

Temperature Conversions

Fahrenheit (°F)	Celsius (°C)
32°F	0°C
212°F	100°C
Formula: (°F - 32) x 0.5556 = °C	Formula: (°C x 1.8) + 32 = °F

Oven Temperature Conversions

US Oven Term	Fahrenheit (°F)	Celsius (°C)
Very Slow	250°F	120°C
Slow	300-325°F	150-165°C
Moderate	350-375°F	175-190°C
Moderately Hot	400°F	200°C
Hot	425-450°F	220-230°C
Very Hot	475-500°F	245-260°C

GLOSSARY OF INGREDIENTS

Acai Berry - *Description:* Small, dark purple berry from the Amazon. Rich in antioxidants and fiber. - *Anti-inflammatory Benefits:* Contains anthocyanins which aid in reducing inflammation.

Adzuki Beans - *Description:* Small, reddish-brown beans, sweet and nutty in flavor. - *Anti-inflammatory Benefits:* High in fiber and protein, supports digestion and reduces inflammation.

Alfalfa Sprouts - *Description:* Tender, crunchy young shoots of the alfalfa plant, often used in salads. - *Anti-inflammatory Benefits:* Provides saponins and can help modulate the immune system.

Allspice - *Description:* Dried unripe berry from the P. dioica tree, resembles the flavor of several spices. - *Anti-inflammatory Benefits:* Contains eugenol, which reduces inflammation and acts as a pain reliever.

Almond Oil - *Description:* Mild, nutty oil derived from almonds. - *Anti-inflammatory Benefits:* Rich in monounsaturated fats, beneficial for heart health and anti-inflammatory effects.

Almonds - *Description:* Nut with a rich flavor, used in a variety of dishes from salads to desserts. - *Anti-inflammatory Benefits:* High in vitamin E, which protects the body from oxidative damage.

Amaranth - *Description:* Gluten-free grain known for its nutritious seeds and leaves. - *Anti-inflammatory Benefits:* Rich in antioxidants and can help reduce inflammation.

Anise - *Description:* Flavorful spice known for its licorice-like flavor. - *Anti-inflammatory Benefits:* Used for treating inflammatory conditions and digestive problems.

Apple - *Description:* Crunchy and sweet fruit, rich in fiber and available in various colors. - *Anti-inflammatory Benefits:* Contains quercetin, an antioxidant that helps reduce inflammation.

Apricot - *Description:* Small, orange fruit with a velvety skin and a sweet, slightly tart flavor. - *Anti-inflammatory Benefits:* Rich in vitamins A and C, which are antioxidants that help fight inflammation.

Artichoke - *Description:* A thistle-like vegetable offering meaty texture in its bulb. - *Anti-inflammatory Benefits:* High in dietary fiber, vitamin C, and flavonoids.

Asparagus - *Description:* Slender stalks harvested in spring, known for their distinct, savory flavor. - *Anti-inflammatory Benefits:* Contains saponins and flavonoids which help reduce inflammatory processes.

Avocado - *Description:* Creamy fruit used in various dishes; rich in healthy fats. - *Anti-inflammatory Benefits:* High in oleic acid, which reduces inflammation and can help lower the risk of heart disease.

Barley - *Description:* Versatile cereal grain with a hearty flavor. - *Anti-inflammatory Benefits:* Offers beta-glucan, which lowers cholesterol and minimizes inflammation.

Basil - *Description:* Sweet-smelling herb often used in Italian and Southeast Asian cooking. - *Anti-inflammatory Benefits:* Contains eugenol, which works as a natural anti-inflammatory agent.

Beet - *Description:* Root vegetable with a vivid red color and earthy taste. - *Anti-inflammatory Benefits:* High in betalains, which have been shown to reduce inflammation and oxidative stress.

Bell Pepper - *Description:* Crunchy vegetable available in various colors, sweet in flavor. - *Anti-inflammatory Benefits:* Rich in vitamin C and antioxidants.

Blueberry - *Description:* Small, sweet, and tart berries with deep blue color. - *Anti-inflammatory Benefits:* Exceptionally high in antioxidants, predominantly anthocyanins, which reduce inflammation.

Broccoli - *Description:* Green vegetable with tree-like florets, related to cabbage and cauliflower. - *Anti-inflammatory Benefits:* Contains sulforaphane, an antioxidant that fights inflammation.

Brussels Sprouts - *Description:* Small, cabbage-like sprouts known for their nutty flavor. - *Anti-inflammatory Benefits:* Rich in antioxidants and helps decrease inflammation markers.

Cabbage - *Description:* Leafy biennial plant, green or purple, used in salads and slaws. - *Anti-inflammatory Benefits:* Includes glutamine and antioxidants with anti-inflammatory properties.

Carrot - *Description:* Root vegetable, typically orange, with a crunchy texture. - *Anti-inflammatory Benefits:* Provides beta-carotene and other antioxidants that reduce inflammation.

Cauliflower - *Description:* White, fluffy vegetable similar to broccoli in shape, but with a milder taste. - *Anti-inflammatory Benefits:* Contains choline and is high in antioxidants like vitamin K.

Celery - *Description:* Long, crunchy stalks often used in soups and salads. - *Anti-inflammatory Benefits:* Offers luteolin, an antioxidant that reduces inflammation and can inhibit the growth of cancer cells.

Cherry - *Description:* Small, round fruit with a pit, ranges from sweet to tart in flavor. - *Anti-inflammatory Benefits:* High in polyphenols and vitamin C, which have been shown to reduce muscle inflammation and pain.

Chia Seeds - *Description:* Tiny, nutrient-packed seeds often used in smoothies or as a yogurt topping. - *Anti-inflammatory Benefits:* Rich in omega-3 fatty acids, which reduce inflammation.

Collard Greens - *Description:* Green leafy vegetable, common in Southern US cuisine. - *Anti-inflammatory Benefits:* High in vitamin A, C, and K, and flavonoids known to diminish inflammation.

Cranberry - *Description:* Tart, red fruit often used in sauces and juices. - *Anti-inflammatory Benefits:* Contains unique proanthocyanidins that prevent bacterial adhesion and reduce inflammation.

Cucumber - *Description:* Long, green fruit typically eaten fresh. - *Anti-inflammatory Benefits:* Hydrating and contains cucurbitacin E, which provides anti-inflammatory effects.

Dandelion Greens - *Description:* Leafy greens from the dandelion plant, slightly bitter in taste. - *Anti-inflammatory Benefits:* Rich in vitamins A, C, and K, and anti-inflammatory compounds.

Dates - *Description:* Sweet fruit from the date palm, chewy in texture. - *Anti-inflammatory Benefits:* Offers magnesium, which helps lower blood pressure.

Eggplant - *Description:* Glossy, purple vegetable, spongy in texture. - *Anti-inflammatory Benefits:* Contains nasunin, a potent antioxidant with anti-inflammatory properties.

Flaxseed Oil - *Description:* A nutritious oil derived from the seeds of the flax plant, high in omega-3 fatty acids. - *Anti-inflammatory Benefits:* Contains ALA, an omega-3 that is converted in the body to EPA and DHA, which are powerful anti-inflammatory substances.

Greek Yogurt - *Description:* A thick, creamy yogurt strained to remove excess moisture, lactose, and sugars. - *Anti-inflammatory Benefits:* Contains probiotics that help maintain gut health, which is crucial for managing inflammation.

Hazelnuts - *Description:* Sweet-flavored nuts, commonly used in baked goods and chocolates. - *Anti-inflammatory Benefits:* High in vitamin E, healthy fats, and proteins, which contribute to reducing inflammation.

Honey - *Description:* A natural sweetener produced by bees foraging nectar from flowers. - *Anti-inflammatory Benefits:* Offers antioxidants like flavonoids and phenolic acids which help reduce inflammation.

Horseradish - *Description:* A pungent root vegetable, often grated and used as a condiment. - *Anti-inflammatory Benefits:* Contains compounds that may help detoxify the body and prevent inflammation.

Jalapeño - *Description:* Small green or red pepper which is mildly spicy. - *Anti-inflammatory Benefits:* Capsaicin, the active component, can ease pain and reduce inflammation.

Jasmine Rice - *Description:* A type of long-grain rice known for its fragrant aroma. - *Anti-inflammatory Benefits:* Offers a good source of energy and can help balance inflammation when mixed with a diet rich in antioxidants.

Kale - *Description:* A type of leafy green vegetable recognized for its curly leaves and earthy taste. - *Anti-inflammatory Benefits:* Loaded with vitamins A, K, and C, as well as antioxidants such as quercetin and kaempferol that combat inflammation.

Kiwi - *Description:* Small, brown, fuzzy fruit with a bright green or golden, sweet, and tangy flesh. - *Anti-inflammatory Benefits:* Rich in vitamin C and other antioxidants that help reduce oxidative stress and inflammation.

Kohlrabi - *Description:* A bulbous vegetable, part of the cabbage family, with a texture and taste similar to a broccoli stem but milder. - *Anti-inflammatory Benefits:* Provides significant amounts of vitamin C and fiber, both known for their anti-inflammatory properties.

Leek - *Description:* A vegetable belonging to the onion family, milder and larger than scallions. - *Anti-inflammatory Benefits:* Contains allicin, which is effective in reducing inflammation and promoting overall health.

Lemon - *Description:* Bright yellow fruit known for its acidic juice. - *Anti-inflammatory Benefits:* Packed with vitamin C, bioflavonoids that strengthen the capillaries and reduce inflammation.

Lentils - *Description:* Small, lens-shaped legumes available in many colors and varieties. - *Anti-inflammatory Benefits:* High in fiber and protein, which can alleviate inflammation and aid in muscle repair.

Lettuce - *Description:* Leafy greens commonly used in salads. Varieties include romaine, iceberg, and butterhead. - *Anti-inflammatory Benefits:* Contains vitamin K and antioxidants that help reduce inflammatory markers in the blood.

Lime - *Description:* Green citrus fruit, usually smaller and more acidic than lemons. - *Anti-inflammatory Benefits:* Offers vitamin C and flavonoids which have strong antioxidant and anti-inflammatory properties.

Lychee - *Description:* Tropical fruit with a rough red outer skin, sweet, fragrant white flesh. - *Anti-inflammatory Benefits:* Apart from vitamin C, it has oligonol which can decrease inflammation and fight fatigue.

Macadamia Nuts - *Description:* Small, buttery-flavored nuts, native to Australia, rich in fats. - *Anti-inflammatory Benefits:* High in monounsaturated fats and low in omega-6 fatty acids, beneficial for reducing inflammation.

Millet - *Description:* A gluten-free ancient grain, often ground into flour or used as a staple in many cultures. - *Anti-inflammatory Benefits:* Contains magnesium which reduces inflammation in conditions like arthritis.

Mint - *Description:* Aromatic herb recognized by its cool, refreshing flavor. - *Anti-inflammatory Benefits:* Contains menthol, which has natural analgesic and anti-inflammatory properties.

Mung Beans - *Description:* Small green beans that cook quickly. Known for their sweet flavor. - *Anti-inflammatory Benefits:* Loaded with nutrients that lower inflammatory markers such as IL-6 and CRP.

Olive Oil - *Description:* Well-known cooking oil derived from olives, staple of the Mediterranean diet. - *Anti-inflammatory Benefits:* Contains oleocanthal, which has been shown to work similarly to ibuprofen in reducing inflammation.

Onion - *Description:* Bulb vegetable used worldwide, known for its sharp taste and smell. - *Anti-inflammatory Benefits:* High in quercetin, a flavonoid antioxidant that inhibits inflammation and acts as an antihistamine.

Orange - *Description:* Popular citrus fruit, known for its bright color and sweet-tart taste. - *Anti-inflammatory Benefits:* Abundant in vitamin C, potassium, and folate, all crucial for reducing inflammation and bolstering immune function.

Oregano - *Description:* A robust herb frequently used in Italian and Mediterranean cuisines. - *Anti-inflammatory Benefits:* Packed with antioxidants, including thymol and rosmarinic acid, which fight free radicals and reduce inflammation.

Oyster Mushrooms - *Description:* Fan-shaped, silky mushrooms known for their delicate texture and mild, savory flavor. - *Anti-inflammatory Benefits:* Contain beta-glucans and antioxidants that help reduce inflammation and promote immunity.

Papaya - *Description:* Tropical fruit with sweet, orange flesh and numerous black seeds. - *Anti-inflammatory Benefits:* Contains papain, an enzyme that aids digestion and reduces inflammation.

Parsley - *Description:* Bright green herb, often used as a garnish, with a fresh, slightly peppery flavor. - *Anti-inflammatory Benefits:* Contains vitamins A, C, and E, which can help control blood pressure and have anti-inflammatory effects.

Parsnip - *Description:* Root vegetable resembling a cream-colored carrot, with a sweet, nutty flavor. - *Anti-inflammatory Benefits:* Rich in fiber and antioxidants, helps to lower blood pressure and fight inflammation.

Peach - *Description:* Soft, juicy fruit with fuzzy skin and sweet flesh. - *Anti-inflammatory Benefits:* Offers vitamins A and C, which help repair tissues and reduce inflammation.

Peanut Oil - *Description:* Mild-tasting oil derived from peanuts, commonly used in cooking. - *Anti-inflammatory Benefits:* High levels of vitamin E and monounsaturated fats aid in reducing inflammation.

Pear - *Description:* Sweet, bell-shaped fruit with a soft, succulent interior. - *Anti-inflammatory Benefits:* High in dietary fiber and vitamin C, aiding in decreasing inflammation levels.

Peas - *Description:* Small, round, green seed typically eaten as a vegetable. - *Anti-inflammatory Benefits:* Contains anti-inflammatory nutrients like vitamin C and omega-3 fats.

Pecans - *Description:* Smooth, buttery nut often used in desserts. - *Anti-inflammatory Benefits:* High in magnesium, which is known for its anti-inflammatory benefits.

Pineapple - *Description:* Tropical fruit with a rough, spiky exterior and sweet, juicy interior. - *Anti-inflammatory Benefits:* High in bromelain, an enzyme that may help manage inflammation, reduce swelling, and aid recovery.

Plum - *Description:* Small fruit with smooth skin and sweet-tart flesh. - *Anti-inflammatory Benefits:* Contains antioxidants and vitamin C that fight oxidative stress and lower inflammation.

Pomegranate - *Description:* Red fruit with a tough outer layer and sweet red seeds inside. - *Anti-inflammatory Benefits:* Loaded with antioxidants, particularly punicalagin thought to reduce inflammation.

Pumpkin Seeds - *Description:* Flat, oval seeds with a chewy texture and nutty flavor. - *Anti-inflammatory Benefits:* High in omega-3 fatty acids and zinc, both of which have strong anti-inflammatory properties.

Pumpkin - *Description:* Large, round orange squash with a thick, ribbed shell. - *Anti-inflammatory Benefits:* High in vitamin A and potassium, which support immunity and reduce inflammation.

Quinoa - *Description:* A pseudo-cereal that cooks like a grain, known for its nutrient richness. - *Anti-inflammatory Benefits:* Provides complete protein with all essential amino acids and is high in anti-inflammatory phytonutrients.

Rosemary - *Description:* Woody herb with needle-like leaves, offering an intense aroma and flavor. - *Anti-inflammatory Benefits:* Contains rosmarinic acid and other antioxidants that help reduce inflammation.

Saffron - *Description:* One of the most expensive spices in the world, derived from the stigmas of crocus flowers. - *Anti-inflammatory Benefits:* Possesses antioxidant properties that can help reduce inflammation and stress.

Sage - *Description:* Grayish herb with a strong, slightly minty flavor. - *Anti-inflammatory Benefits:* Full of anti-inflammatory and antioxidant compounds that can reduce the risk of chronic diseases.

Sesame Oil - *Description:* Derived from sesame seeds, this oil is used extensively in Asian cooking. - *Anti-inflammatory Benefits:* Contains sesamol, which is known for its anti-inflammatory and antioxidant properties.

Thyme - *Description:* Small, pungent Mediterranean herb used in a variety of cuisines. - *Anti-inflammatory Benefits:* Contains thymol, an antimicrobial essential oil that reduces inflammation and protects against chronic diseases.

Trout - *Description:* Freshwater fish with a mild, nutty flavor. - *Anti-inflammatory Benefits:* Rich in omega-3 fatty acids, which are crucial for reducing inflammation throughout the body.

Tuna - *Description:* Predatory saltwater fish often canned or sold fresh. - *Anti-inflammatory Benefits:* High in omega-3 fats, beneficial for reducing heart inflammation and improving cardiovascular health.

Turmeric - *Description:* A bright yellow-orange spice often used in curries and sauces. - *Anti-inflammatory Benefits:* Contains curcumin, a chemical that significantly reduces inflammation in the body.

Ugli Fruit - *Description:* A citrus fruit known for its rough, wrinkled, greenish-yellow skin, combining the tastes of grapefruit, orange, and tangerine. - *Anti-inflammatory Benefits:* Rich in vitamin C, it boosts the immune system and reduces inflammation.

Vanilla - *Description:* Derived from orchids of the genus Vanilla, used as flavoring in a variety of products. - *Anti-inflammatory Benefits:* Antioxidant properties help prevent the breakdown of cells and tissues.

Walnut Oil - *Description:* Oil extracted from walnuts, known for its rich, nutty flavor. - *Anti-inflammatory Benefits:* High in polyunsaturated fatty acids and antioxidants that help reduce inflammation.

Walnuts - *Description:* Round, single-seeded stone fruits of the walnut tree. - *Anti-inflammatory Benefits:* Rich in omega-3 fatty acids, which are essential for reducing inflammation.

Wasabi - *Description:* Japanese horseradish that provides a sharp, pungent flavor to sushi and other dishes. - *Anti-inflammatory Benefits:* The isothiocyanates in wasabi help reduce inflammation and inhibit bacterial growth.

Watercress - *Description:* An aquatic leafy green vegetable grown in natural spring water. - *Anti-inflammatory Benefits:* It's packed with antioxidants that support reducing oxidative stress and inflammation.

Wheat Germ Oil - *Description:* Extracted from the germ of the wheat kernel. - *Anti-inflammatory Benefits:* High in vitamin E, which is known for reducing inflammation and protecting the body from free radicals.

Wheatgrass - *Description:* The freshly sprouted first leaves of the wheat plant, used as a food, drink, or dietary supplement. - *Anti-inflammatory Benefits:* High in chlorophyll, vitamins A, C, and E, it cleanses the body and combats inflammation.

Wild Rice - *Description:* A species of grass that produces edible seeds resembling rice. - *Anti-inflammatory Benefits:* Contains compounds that can help lower inflammation and improve heart health.

Xigua - *Description:* Commonly known as the watermelon, xigua is rich in water and nutrients. - *Anti-inflammatory Benefits:* Contains lycopene and cucurbitacin E which provide anti-inflammatory benefits.

Xylitol - *Description:* A sugar alcohol used as a sweetener. - *Anti-inflammatory Benefits:* Xylitol can reduce bacteria in the mouth, preventing inflammation in dental tissues.

Yam - *Description:* A tuber vegetable resembling a sweet potato, but with more starch and dryness. - *Anti-inflammatory Benefits:* High in vitamin C and beta-carotene, helps to reduce inflammation.

Yellowtail - *Description:* A popular fish in Japanese cuisine, known for its tender, white flesh and mild flavor. - *Anti-inflammatory Benefits:* Rich in omega-3 fatty acids, beneficial for heart health and reducing inflammation.

Yerba Mate - *Description:* A type of tea made from the leaves and twigs of the Ilex paraguariensis plant. - *Anti-inflammatory Benefits:* Contains saponins, which are natural anti-inflammatories and can help reduce the risk of chronic diseases.

Yogurt - *Description:* A dairy product made by fermenting milk with a yogurt culture. - *Anti-inflammatory Benefits:* Contains probiotics that promote healthy digestion and reduce inflammation in the gut.

Za'atar - *Description:* A Middle Eastern spice blend made from dried herbs, sesame seeds, dried sumac, and salt. - *Anti-inflammatory Benefits:* The herbs in za'atar are high in antioxidants and have anti-inflammatory properties.

Zander - *Description:* A type of freshwater fish similar to perch. - *Anti-inflammatory Benefits:* Provides a good source of omega-3 fatty acids, which are known to reduce inflammation.

Zucchini - *Description:* Also known as courgette, a summer squash which can reach nearly a meter in length. - *Anti-inflammatory Benefits:* Its high antioxidant content may help to reduce inflammation.

RESOURCES FOR FURTHER READING

Embarking on a journey to a healthier lifestyle through anti-inflammatory eating is akin to sitting down with a book whose pages are not yet written — you hold the pen. And as every writer cherishes a library that guides and inspires them, so should you have resources that broaden your knowledge and understanding of how food can heal and energize.

Imagine a cozy armchair by a large window, a cup of herbal tea steaming gently beside a stack of books. These aren't just any books; these are your companions for the journey towards wellness. Each one opens up new ways of understanding your dietary choices and their impacts. I've always believed that a well-chosen book can act almost like a wise old friend, offering advice, wisdom, and, occasionally, a new perspective that challenges your assumptions.

Let's start this exploration with Dr. Cassandra Parks. She is a renowned nutritionist whose revolutionary work, **"Inflammation and You: A New Approach"**, dives deep into the physiological processes of inflammation and explains how certain foods can either exacerbate or alleviate these conditions. Dr. Parks uses vivid, real-life anecdotes to make complex biological concepts relatable. Her book is a guide that intertwines scientific insight with personal stories, showing the profound impact diet can have on our health.

Next, consider an evening spent with Michael Stanton's **"The Anti-Inflammation Cookbook: Meals That Heal."** This isn't just a recipe collection, but a narrative journey through cultures that have used natural, wholesome foods to fight disease for centuries. Michael's travel encounters and interviews with local healers enrich his recipes with context, making every dish a tale of discovery and recovery.

In the realm of practical wisdom, **"The Quick Start Guide to Anti-Inflammatory Eating"** by Lara Thompson provides a straightforward, no-frills approach that's perfect for someone just beginning their health journey. Lara, a former professional chef turned nutritional therapist, breaks down the anti-inflammatory diet into simple, adaptable steps. She understands the challenges of a busy life and provides solutions that cater not just to your health, but also to your time.

For those who are visually inclined, Jane Edwards' **"A Visual Guide to Anti-Inflammatory Foods"** is a beautifully illustrated book that details the health benefits of diverse foods in vivid colors and images. It's a feast for your eyes and a treasure for your kitchen counter, providing quick references and sparking joy and motivation each time you glance its way.

When it comes to the science behind the diet, **"Flames of Healing: The Science Behind Anti-Inflammatory Foods"** by Dr. Henry Gail is a must-read. Dr. Gail's methodical approach will appeal to those who have a keen interest in understanding the biochemical interactions between different foods and our body's inflammatory pathways. His detailed analysis is complemented by case studies that trace the journeys of individuals who have transformed their lives through dietary changes.

No resource list is complete without touching upon the stories of everyday heroes. **"True Stories of Dietary Transformation"** compiles several heartening stories from real people who have turned their lives around by making conscious food choices. Compiled by Angela Field, this collection shows that change is possible and within reach; each story is a testament to the power of persistence and knowledge.

To keep our knowledge in tune with the latest scientific advancements, **"Current Trends in Anti-Inflammatory Diets"**, a yearly publication by the Institute of Health and Nutrition, offers insights into the ongoing research and emerging trends in nutrition science. It serves not just as a reading material but as a bridge connecting us to the frontline of dietary science and innovation.

In soothing tones and rich detail, these books and publications pave a path through the thicket of misinformation and complexity. They inspire, educate, and, most importantly, they empower. Whether you're someone who's looking to overhaul your diet completely or just make more informed choices, each of these resources offers something valuable.

As you continue to write your story of health and wellness, remember that these books are more than just collections of words on a page. They are a support network, a series of guideposts that light your way as you navigate the sometimes challenging but always rewarding path toward a healthier life.

Every journey is unique, and so is every reader. Whether you seek scientific validation, inspirational stories, or practical advice, these resources are here to support your personal narrative. They are here to reassure you that while the journey towards a healthier life through mindful eating isn't always easy, it is indeed possible and well worth the effort. Each page turned is a step forward, each book finished a chapter written in your own journey of wellness. Embrace these resources, allow them to guide you, and watch as your own pages fill with stories of success and vibrant health.

A SPECIAL THANK YOU

Dear Reader,

Thank you so much for purchasing my **"Anti-Inflammatory Cookbook for Beginners 2024."**

Your journey towards better health and wellness is incredibly important to me, and I am thrilled to be a part of it. I hope you find the recipes delicious, easy to follow, and effective in reducing inflammation and energizing your life.

Your feedback is invaluable to me. If you enjoyed this cookbook, I would greatly appreciate it if you could take a moment to leave an honest review on Amazon.

Your insights help me improve and assist other readers in making informed choices. Reviews are the lifeblood of my efforts, and your support means the world to me.

As a token of my appreciation, I have a special bonus just for you!
I am excited to offer you an exclusive eBook, **"Workout Guide for Reducing Inflammation."**
This comprehensive guide includes yoga, stretching routines, and low-impact workouts specifically designed to help reduce inflammation and enhance your overall well-being.

To download your free bonus eBook, simply scan the QR code below. I hope this additional resource helps you on your journey to achieving a balanced and healthy lifestyle.

Thank you once again for your support and trust. I wish you all the best on your path to wellness and look forward to hearing about your experiences.

With gratitude,

Zelda Fleming

SCAN QR CODE TO DOWNLOAD YOUR BONUS

Made in United States
Orlando, FL
14 March 2025